THE
LITTLE
BOOK
OF
YOUGHAL

KIERAN GROEGER

First published 2016

The History Press Ireland
50 City Quay
Dublin 2
Ireland
www.thehistorypress.ie

The History Press Ireland are a member of Publishing Ireland,
the Irish Book Publisher's Association.

British Library Cataloguing in Publication Data.
A catalogue record for this book is available from the British Library.

ISBN 978 1 84588 342 3

Typesetting and origination by The History Press
Printed and bound by TJ International Ltd.

CONTENTS

ACKNOWLEDGEMENTS

To Beth Amphlett and The History Press Ireland for inviting me to write this book.

To Kieran Wyse and the staff of Cork County Library, Marian O'Halloran and the staff of Youghal Library, Brian McGee and staff at Cork City and County Archives.

To David Kelly for his amazing wealth of knowledge about Youghal.

To Michaeli and Helen Waide for their help.

To Michael Hackett for all his wonderful books about the town.

To the staff at Community Radio Youghal for their help.

To all who have offered advice and suggestions for topics and themes, especially to Dagmar O'Riain-Raedel and all the Youghal Celebrates History conferences which have been ruthlessly pillaged in the writing of this book.

To Aonghus O'Broin for proofreading the text.

To my wife Brid for her support and patience.

To all of you a sincere 'Thank you'.

INTRODUCTION

Some towns just ... happen. One day you wouldn't dream of the place as a suitable location, the next day it is perfect. It just happens! Youghal happened. The majestic River Blackwater broke its banks during a big storm in the early ninth century and found a new, more direct way to the sea. It used to meander slowly to what is today called Whiting Bay. The name in Irish ('*Beal an Abha*' or 'mouth of the river') tells the story. Whiting Bay is between Youghal and Ardmore. Today, the old riverbed has dried up but is still visible.

Suddenly on the western side of the river there was a fine area for Vikings to drag up their boats, to build a settlement, to protect it with walls and to build a church. There were fine vantage points where lookouts could be posted and a small community began to develop along the old '*Bealcah Eo Chaill*' – the old Yew Wood Way. Youghal came into existence. It just happened.

The history of the town, as a town, can be attributed to a handful of people, in two main categories – those before and those after Walter Raleigh, whose image stands in the middle of the town, straddling the old world and the new. This is the opinion of Professor Tadhg O'Keeffe of UCD. The first period is dominated by the Fitzgerald dynasty, who took over an enormous segment of land for themselves (some 500,000 acres). They became totally dominant and increasingly independent of the English monarchy, which began to try to rein them in. Finally, a rebellion by the Fitzgeralds was ruthlessly and efficiently stamped out. Their land was given to English adventurers, soldiers and landlords, who were for the most part Protestant. From then on religion would also play a part in the history of Ireland.

Approximately 40,000 acres were given to Walter Raleigh for his part in stamping out the rebellion. He stayed for a while but found it impossible to make money from the land. He had difficulties attracting English settlers, difficulties getting a licence to export timber and difficulties paying tax. The country had been devastated and depopulated by the Fitzgerald rebellion. He sold his land to Richard Boyle. This begins the second half of the town's history, when a loyal and predominantly Protestant group try to maintain a vice-like grip on the town, despite an ever-increasing population of Catholics who are necessary traders and workers in the town and who begin to demand basic civil rights.

Boyle's descendants retained control over the Raleigh estate and the town of Youghal, almost until the Free State of Ireland was formed, in the early twentieth century At one stage there was no male Boyle inheritor, so the land went to the Cavendish family (Dukes of Devonshire) who still hold fishing rights, hunting rights and a substantial amount of land in the area.

Major trouble blew up in 1641, which is referred to in the *Annals of Youghal* as the 'Great Rebellion'. Richard Boyle and his sons played a major role in suppressing it, as did Admiral Penn and Oliver Cromwell, who eventually systematically and ruthlessly crushed all resistance to the armed forces of the English Parliament.

Catholic hopes resurfaced in 1660, when the Stuart monarchy was restored. Catholics hoped for some restoration of their own rights and lands. For a short while there was a Catholic mayor and council in Youghal, but the defeat of King James at the Battle of the Boyne put an end to Catholic aspirations, although some hope lingered during the eighteenth century in the poetry of the people – as the poems of Piaras Mac Gearailt (1709–92) show, especially in his '*Rosc Catha na Mumhan*' (the Battle Cry of Munster) a longing for the arrival of Bonny Prince Charlie and a better deal for his Catholic subjects.

In 1798 there was another rebellion, mainly in Wexford, but there was some trouble in Youghal.

In the nineteenth century Youghal saw the struggle for Catholic Emancipation. Daniel O'Connell's son John became a Member of Parliament for Youghal. Events in Youghal included a campaign to repeal the Act of Union, the Great Famine, the Land War, the arrival of the railway, and a major economic bubble, which had a spectacular burst! And then in the twentieth century there was another boom, this time with the textile industry followed by another burst and another …

Youghal struggled on, always boom followed by bust. This is the story of Youghal.

1

MAJOR EVENTS

1500 BC – The Castlerichard Urn discovered near Youghal in 1968, probably made from local clay around this date.

575 AD – St Coran the wise founded a baptistery at a place called 'Shanavine' (Old Sanctuary). He is remembered in place names like Kilcoran Road. His feast day is celebrated on 9 February. There were early-Christian settlements in the area from this time.

812 AD – The Danes arrived and sailed up the River Blackwater as far as Lismore. Both Danes and Norwegians invaded Ireland from the ninth century.

830 AD – Following a storm the River Blackwater broke its banks, creating a new entry into the sea. The previous entry point for the river is now called Whiting Bay, but the name in Irish (*Beal an Abha* or mouth of the river) reveals its true history.

853 AD – Sigtrygg the Viking built a fort at the new mouth of the river. It quickly grew and developed into a bustling port. By the thirteenth century many settlers would come to Youghal, especially from Bristol.

1155 – Pope Adrian IV with his letter *Laudabiliter* allowed King Henry II of England to take over Ireland. From this time English monarchs claimed Ireland as part of their kingdom.

1177 – King Henry granted land in Munster to Robert Fitzstephen who, in turn, gave the land in south Munster (called 'Desmond' from the Irish '*Deas Mumha*' or south Munster) to his half brother Maurice Fitzgerald, ancestor of the Earls of Desmond. The Fitzgerald family would dominate south Munster for almost 400 years.

1220 –   Services began in the Chapel of St Mary in Youghal and have continued to the present day. From that day to the present there has been an unbroken line of priests, ministers and rectors.

1224 –   The Franciscans established an abbey at Youghal, followed soon after by the Dominicans (1268) and the Benedictines (1350). The Augustinians arrived about forty years before the Franciscans and were based at Molana Abbey.

1302 –   Stephen O'Regan was assaulted by John Don leading to a court case.

1317 –   Roger Mortimer, Lord of Meath and Chief Justice of Ireland landed at Youghal with a large army and thirty-eight knights, forcing Edward Bruce to retreat.

1348 –   The Black Death visited Youghal, wiping out half the population. Like many port towns, Youghal suffered attacks from the plague intermittently, the last outbreak being in 1651.

1404 –   Youghal was under constant attack by rebels.

1462 –   Youghal became one of the 'cinque ports' of Ireland. The increased trade led to a big increase in the number of pirates operating around the coast.

1464 –   A college was established by Thomas Fitzgerald, Eighth Earl of Desmond. The college was to train priests for the church. St Mary's became a collegiate church, one of the first university colleges in Ireland.

1577 –   A Jesuit school was established in Youghal. Dominic Collins, a Jesuit monk, attended there.

1579 –   The Earl of Desmond captured Youghal and ransacked the town for four days.

1583 –   The rebellion of the Earl of Desmond failed and the process of dividing up his land began.

1584 –   Youghal Council applied for the county of Cork to be divided into two, with one half being County Cork and the other County Youghal.

1602 –   On 15 June Dominic Collins was brought to his hometown to be executed. Collins was beatified by Pope John-Paul II in September 1992.

1602 –   Walter Raleigh sold 42,000 acres of land to Richard Boyle for £1,500 The sale included the towns of Youghal, Cappoquin and Lismore.

1604 – The Olde Countess of Desmond died and was buried at South Abbey, with her Fitzgerald ancestors.

1612 – Robert Tynte married Elizabeth Spencer (*née* Boyle). She was the widow of Edmund Spencer. Tynte's castle still remains in the centre of town.

1620 – Richard Boyle was created first Earl of Cork. He also acquired other titles, Baron of Youghal, Viscount of Dungarvan and Lord High Treasurer of Ireland. Five of his sons became earls.

1623 – A pirate called John Nutt captured a man fishing in a little boat off Youghal, while another pirate called Fleming was hanged from the Clock Gate.

1628 – Boyle sold four million pipe staves, exporting some 1,800 tons of them. A cargo vessel of the time, called a 'lighter', could carry fourteen tons of pipe staves, that meant about 1,300 individual journeys by sea to ship out that amount of pipe staves.

1631 – Baltimore was sacked by pirates.

164–1 – Catholics outnumbered other citizens of Youghal by about three to one.

1642 – Four of Richard Boyle's sons fought in the Battle of Liscannor. One of them, Kynalmeaky, was killed.

1643 – Richard Boyle died in Youghal in his house, *The College*.

1644 – Roger Boyle ordered that all Catholics be driven out of Youghal.

1645 – Admiral Penn and three ships were sent to Youghal to break a blockade of the harbour by the forces of Lord Castlehaven.

1649 – In December, Oliver Cromwell arrived in Youghal and left Ireland the following May, from Youghal on board his ship the *President*, bound for Bristol.

1661 – The trial, in Youghal, of Florence Newton for witchcraft

1689 – Colonel Congreve was commander of the garrison.

1690 – The arrival of a number of French Huguenots to Youghal, fleeing persecution in France.

1753 – The Boyle family had no male heirs and the estate passed to the Cavendish family.

1759 – Piaras Mac Gearailt (Fitzgerald), famous poet, with a very heavy heart 'went up the hill', in other words he became a Protestant.

1757 – Birth of miniature-portrait artist Samson Towgood Roch in Youghal.

1762 – A series of outrages began in counties Cork, Waterford and Tipperary by a group of men who put white shirts over their clothes, ostensibly, as some form of disguise, hence their name Whiteboys.

1765 – John Wesley visited Youghal and preached in St Mary's Collegiate Church.

1777 – The present Clock Gate was built.

1780 – Lord Edward Fitzgerald, a lieutenant in the 96th Regiment of Foot was stationed in Youghal.

1787 – Prince William Henry, later to be King William IV, visited Youghal as commander of his ship the *Pegasus*.

1795 – Arthur Wellesley, later Duke of Wellington, spent the winter in Youghal. He was then a colonel in the Thirty-Third Infantry, waiting for a suitable moment to sail to Guadaloupe.

1796 – A 'Fata Morgana' (a superior sort of mirage in the sky) was seen in Youghal and further instances were reported in the *Annals* in two other years.

1796 – A relaxation of the Penal Laws enabled the building of St Mary's parish church, the first Catholic church to be built in the dioceses since the Reformation.

1798 – There was a major rebellion in Ireland with help from France.

1815 – Youghal began to decline after the ending of the Napoleonic wars.

1825 – Youghal Library was built.

1832 – Police force introduced to Youghal, initially a constable and five men.

1835 – John O'Connell, son of Daniel O'Connell was elected MP for Youghal.

1846 – The Great Famine. There were riots in Youghal as starving people demanded food.

1849 – Cholera hit Youghal and there were forty deaths.

1852 – Isaac Butt was elected Member of Parliament for Youghal, winning by two votes.

1865 –   Isaac Butt was defeated by J.N. McKenna.

1860 –   The railway line from Cork to Youghal was opened.

1867 –   Year of the Fenian Rising, Knockadoon Coastguard station was captured by the Fenians and Michael O'Brien from Ladysbridge was hanged in Manchester, being one of the 'Manchester Martyrs'.

1881 –   James Connolly served with the King's Liverpool Regiment, stationed in Youghal.

1882 –   Talbot Ponsonby offered to sell his estate to a London consortium.

1883 –   The new iron bridge over the river was built.

1883 –   Stones were thrown at soldiers and reinforcements escorted them back to barracks.

1888 –   An attempt to hold a monster protest meeting in Youghal was stopped by the police and army.

1890 –   The army and police evicted twelve more families on the Ponsonby estate. All had joined the Plan of Campaign.

1921 –   During the Irish War of Independence an IRA landmine on the outskirts of Youghal killed seven and injured several soldiers of the Royal Hampshire Regiment.

1922 –   Civil War in Ireland, the *Helga* landed her troops and took over Youghal.

1947 –   Seafield Fabrics opened in Youghal by Minister Sean Lemass.

1950 –   William Trevor (author) lived in Youghal and attended the local Loreto Primary School.

1953 –   An Tostal Festival began in Youghal.

2006 –   A new Community School opened in Youghal, combining all three second-level schools in one new building. A whole new era was starting.

2014 –   Youghal Town Council and the office of mayor were abolished, bringing 800 years of local government to an end.

2

PEOPLE

WALTER RALEIGH

Raleigh is the single link which connects the old Irish, Gaelic, Catholic world with the new modern, English Protestant world. He is not the most significant person in the history of the town but he straddles these two worlds.

There are many questions about Raleigh or was it Rawley, Rauley or Ralegh? (He himself never wrote his name as Raleigh.) Did he have an illegitimate child in Youghal? Why was he executed? Why was he loved by ordinary English people and so hated by rivals in the court? Did he really put his cloak on the ground so that a coquette queen might not get her toes dirty? Why did he hate Catholics so much? Was he a pirate, poet, patron of the arts, lover of the esoteric and the black arts, a dreamer of dreams, scientist, shipbuilder, loving husband and womaniser, friend of Shakespeare, Spencer and Marlowe and almost every significant Elizabethan? Did he really see the St Bartholomew's Day massacre in Paris? Why did King James I hate him and mock him (Really! Rawley?) and eventually have him executed? Was it because of tobacco? Or was Raleigh just a minor gambit on the chessboard of international politics?

You would need to answer all these questions and a few more to understand him but there is not enough time or space to do more than outline some of his career in this *Little Book of Youghal*. There are lots of books to read if you want fuller answers. His was an eventful life and his time in Ireland is but a very brief chapter, although Pope Hennessy devotes a full book to his stay in Ireland.

In Ireland his memory is certainly clouded by the very actions that brought him to public notice – his participation in the massacre of some 600 men, women and children after they had surrendered at Smerwick. The massacre was led by Raleigh and reports of his action went straight to the Queen who 'noticed' her brave young hero. And the more the story was told in *Hooker's Chronicles*, the greater his role became – from a brief mention to a dashing, brave hero. His eight horsemen and eighty foot soldiers were soon challenging hundreds of 'rebels' and he became, to the Queen, 'Our beloved Sir Walter Rawley'.

Raleigh had come to Ireland in 1580 to fight in what became a bitter religious struggle – on one side, the Fitzgerald family, their supporters and some troops from Italy and Spain sent to bolster what was seen as an Irish Catholic rebellion against English Protestant forces. Both sides fought fiercely.

Raleigh arranged the assassination of Gaelic chiefs, tried to stir up trouble with loyal Irish – anything that might show himself in a favourable light, and eventually the superior might and cunning of the English forces prevailed and Munster lay in ruins. Desolate. Decimated. People were left to scavenge corpses just to stay alive, as described by Edmund Spenser:

> Out of every corner of the woods and glens they came creeping forth on their hands, for their legs could not bear them; they looked like anatomies of death; they spake like ghosts crying out of their graves; they did eat the dead carrions, happy where they could find them; yes, and one another soon after, insomuch as the very carcasses they spared not to scrape out of their graves.

The Fitzgerald lands were confiscated – around 600,000 acres – and given to the victorious armies. Raleigh got about 42,000 acres around Youghal, but he wanted more land!

David Edwards, addressing the Youghal Celebrates History conference in 2005, pointed out just how devious Raleigh was. He wanted Barryscourt Castle (just outside Carrigtwohill), Fota Island and the land around Cobh. This would have controlled Cork Harbour and made him wealthy. He had the owners of Barryscourt Castle arrested even though they were loyal. In his letters home he says he 'recovered the castle' but it was never in rebel hands, the owners were actually loyal subjects. A very sneaky character was

Raleigh! He wanted wealth and wanted it fast. Ireland does not 'do' fast, as many invaders found out.

He ordered the knocking down of the North Abbey in Youghal. He ordered the cutting down of thousands of trees along the River Blackwater – to be exported to England. But his enemies made sure he was not allowed to export. He brought in English Protestants to colonise the land. He wanted rents fast. He wanted, in particular, former soldiers who would provide a stout defence of the town if needed. But neither the rents nor enough colonists materialised.

Not enough English came over to Ireland. He could not get an export licence for his timber. He could not get rent from his lands. The surveyors found it almost impossible to accurately survey the land:

> It hath been exceedingly difficult and painful, by reason that the lands having being long waste, are generally overgrown with deep grass, and in most places with heath, brambles and furze, and by the extremity of rain and foul weather, we have been greatly hindered in our proceedings.

But neither the rents nor enough colonists arrived. He began to owe more and more in taxes. Richard Boyle came to his aid by buying his estate from him. The estate only cost Boyle £1,500 but it was not the bargain many people think it was as Boyle also took on the debts of the estate. Raleigh could not manage the estate, he had huge debts and was thrilled to hand it over.

Raleigh was not the man to patiently wait for crops to grow. Some men are hunters and farmers, but he was not a farmer! He wanted instant success – he wanted to find a city of gold – an El Dorado. His pride, his vanity, his superior intellect began to be the cause of his undoing. He never saw the possibility of people he openly despised actually overcoming him.

At his trial, for treason, they actually 'thou'd' him. 'Thou' is the word a lord uses to his inferiors – we don't use it a lot except for one Lord who says 'Thou shalt not kill'. It has the kind of effect the word '*tu*' has on French people if misused. It is an insult to 'thou' someone. So they 'thou'd' him, treated him as if he was an inferior person and he knew the game was up.

He began to write his last will and testament and remembered a certain Alice Goold, in Ireland, with whom he was supposed to have fathered a daughter: 'To my reputed daughter begotten on the body of Alice Goold now in Ireland – 500 marks.' He even wrote to his wife to ask her to be charitable to her and 'teach thy sonne to love her for his father's sake'.

Another of the legends about Raleigh in Youghal concerns the smoking of a pipe of tobacco. Local legends say his servant boy spotted smoke coming out of his mouth and, fearing the worst, threw a bucket of water over him! A bawdier version of that legend has the maid (or Alice Goold) throwing the bucket of water over him, his 'pipe' considered to be a bit of a euphemism and, as the legend goes: 'she hoped the water would diminish his ardour but only succeeded in making it harder!'

He spent long years in the Tower of London under sentence of death but was given permission to go on an expedition to find the mythical El Dorado and it, too, failed. He called to Youghal on the way and Boyle gave him a present of thirty-two gallons of whiskey which he had distilled in Youghal – the first Irish whiskey to be exported to America.

Raleigh's last voyage was a disaster and, on his return, he found himself again in the Tower of London. At the venerable age of 66 he got the chop, or chops really as a clearly overawed executioner made a mess of the execution. There were actually three chops.

Maybe the neck was like 66-year-old leather from his time at sea. He is buried in St Margaret's in London, just next to the Houses of Parliament. It is a beautiful church with a fine stained-glass window depicting episodes from his life. Raleigh's wife was given his head which she kept with her for the rest of her life in a little velvet bag. As you do!

DOMINIC COLLINS (1566–1602)

Dominic Collins was born in Youghal in 1566. His father John Collins, a Catholic, was mayor of the town in 1575. Dominic attended the local Jesuit school. He left Ireland to fight in the wars of religion in France, first on the side of the Duke of Mercoeur and later he joined the garrison at La Corunna in Spain, but then decided he wanted to have a religious life, so he became a Jesuit monk.

In Ireland the Nine Years War was underway as Hugh O'Neill and Hugh O'Donnell had revolted in Ulster. King Philip III of Spain decided to send an army to help them in 1601. An Irish Jesuit, Father James Archer, who was acting as O'Neill's envoy with Rome and Spain, asked that Dominic, who knew the needs of soldiers, and the lie of the land, be sent with him to Ireland. The rebellion was mainly in Ulster, but the Spanish landed in Kinsale on the opposite end of Ireland. The Battle of Kinsale ended the Nine Years War.

Dominic Collins and a handful of men under O'Sullivan Beare took refuge in Dunboy Castle on the Beara Peninsula in West Cork. They were quickly surrounded by Sir George Carew and approximately 4,000 men. Gradually the 143 defenders dwindled in number and Collins offered to try to negotiate a truce. Carew refused to negotiate. The defenders surrendered. There were about sixty soldiers left at that point. All were hanged, except for three who were reserved for interrogation. Two were executed in Cork. Dominic Collins was brought to his hometown of Youghal, perhaps in the hope that pressure might force him to give up his beliefs and save his family the ignominy of a pubic execution. Collins refused and was marched through the streets of Youghal to the spot where the execution would take place. It is marked today by a plaque on the wall. The execution posed a problem when the hangman refused to do his job. With a little 'gentle' persuasion and the suggestion that a failure to cooperate might result in swapping places, a local fisherman acted as hangman. Dominic Collins died proudly proclaiming his faith and became a martyr on 31 October 1602.

WILLIAM SHAKESPEARE

Did Shakespeare really visit Youghal? It is probably impossible to prove conclusively whether he did or not, but there are several reasons for believing that he did.

The harbour master for Youghal was Thomas Shakspere from Bristol. That name, as with Shakespeare himself and with Walter Raleigh, changed spelling a few times before it became the version we have today. Raleigh almost certainly would have spotted the connection between the harbour master's name and his friend William Shakespeare. The Shakespeare family lived on in east Cork until the 1960s. So that is one connection ... but not conclusive evidence.

Walter Raleigh and Shakespeare were friends. Undoubtedly Raleigh, being the peacock that he was, would have loved to show off his friendship with Shakespeare to those in Ireland and would have been proud to strut around Youghal as mayor of the town and owner of a vast estate of land to let his friends in England know that he had become enormously successful in Ireland. Three times Shakespeare's theatre company played in Youghal. There was such a demand to get in that the windows of the theatre were broken. Elizabethan drama groups were regular visitors, taking a ship at Bristol to cross over to Youghal. Richard Boyle paid for the journey the third time. Certainly Shakespeare was not with the company on that third occasion as he had left the Players by then. The first two times, he probably was with them when they came to Youghal. He became very familiar with Irish music, Irish accents and Irish expressions. There are eleven Irish songs in his plays. After the first of these suggested visits Shakespeare put a 'stage Irishman' in his play *Henry V*. He was Captain MacMorrish, the first ever stage Irishman in a play. He has a distinctly Irish accent: 'By Christ, law, tish ill done! The work ish give over, the trumpet sound the retreat. By my hand I swear, and my father's soul, the work ish ill done.'

It is a lovely interpretation of an Irish accent and really could only have been possible if Shakespeare had heard the Irish accent. He uses phrases like 'howling like Irish wolves' – not just wolves but 'Irish wolves', which suggests he knew the difference. 'Coriolanus – gets not just a welcome but 'One hundred thousand welcomes' ('*Cead mile failte*' is the Irish welcome).

One has to wonder if Shakespeare was aware when he picked a hawk for his coat of arms that the Irish word for hawk was '*Seabhac*', pronounced much like Shakespeare might have pronounced the first syllable of his name. The coat of arms involves a hawk and a spear, a '*seabhac*' and a spear. Perhaps an awareness of the Irish language is not proof, *but* there are even more compelling reasons to link Shakespeare with Youghal, as Mary Leland points out in her *Journeys through Literary Cork*.

The Mayor of Youghal was called Francis Annyas, considered by historians to be the first Jewish mayor in the British Isles. His daughter, Sarah, married a Portuguese doctor called Rodrigo Lopez, later to be physician to Queen Elizabeth I. Lopez was the Jew Shakespeare based Shylock on. Lopez was executed for attempting to poison the Queen – a charge he considered to be false and really based on the fact that he was Jewish. His last words – that everyone knew he loved the Lord Jesus just as much as he loved the Queen did not satisfy his accusers who understood the double meaning and off went his head.

In Barton's book *Links between Ireland and Shakespeare* he suggests there are a lot of reasons for believing that Shakespeare did visit Youghal but that he was missing some extra little piece of information to make a definitive conclusion. He seems to have omitted some vital pieces of information.

Raleigh is considered to be central to a group of people referred to as the *School of Night*, a group which included Thomas Harriott, Christopher Marlowe and William Shakespeare. Raleigh is supposed to have presided over this 'school of atheism' in which scholars denied God. Meetings in Youghal were held at an old druid centre near Molana Abbey – where Harriott lived. Raleigh left his 'black suits of apparel' to Harriott in his will. Harriott is one extra link which connects Shakespeare with Youghal.

So did Shakespeare visit Youghal? We never will know for certain but it is likely. Why not?

THOMAS HARRIOTT (1560–1621)

Harriott has never received the true credit for his life's work. He it was who discovered 'openauk' and 'uppowok' (potatoes and tobacco to you and me), brought them to London where Walter Raleigh introduced them to Queen Elizabeth I. Raleigh was not part of that voyage of discovery. He was in England the whole time! Turtle Bunbury grew up near Molana Abbey and explains the story very well in his website.

Harriott was an amazing genius with an interest in mathematics, optics, navigation and ship design. He learnt some of the Indian languages and used a telescope to draw a picture of the moon several months before Galileo. When Raleigh received the land around Youghal he gave one section (around Molana Abbey) to his friend Harriott, who stayed for a while and then moved back to London where he died in 1621.

While living in Molana he discovered the ancient druidic history of the place and local legends suggest the Raleigh, Shakespeare and Marlowe attended meetings there.

He published little and what was published is mostly lost. He was sufficiently important to be attacked by others in print, was accused of atheism and, worse still, suggesting that there were people on earth more than 4,000 years earlier than when Adam was supposed to be alive. Harriott did not accept that the earth was only a few thousand years old. He even wondered about life and death and whether it would be better or not to exist at all or as his friend Shakespeare phrased it: 'To be or not to be, that is the question'.

THE OLDE COUNTESS

When Walter Raleigh was granted over 40,000 acres around Youghal the land included Inchiquin Castle and the domain around it. The lady living in the castle appealed the loss of her land, claiming the land was part of her dowry and that she was entitled to live on the estate. She won her case. The court ruled that she was entitled to live on the land during her life but that the estate would go to Raleigh on her death.

Raleigh accepted the decision of the court but tried to sell her land at one price with her 'in situ' or at another price when she was dead ... which had to be very soon, he believed, given her tremendous age. There are many local legends about the lady.

Very briefly the legends tell us that Katherine Fitzgerald was born in 1464 in Dromana House on the River Blackwater. She was the daughter of Sir John Fitzgerald and she married a cousin – Thomas Fitzgerald (third son of Thomas, the Eighth Earl of Desmond) who was known as 'Baldy Tom' and who died in 1530. For many years she lived as a widow in the castle at Inchiquin, walked regularly into Youghal, sometimes with her daughter. She lost her land to

Sir Walter Raleigh after the Desmond Rebellion, but on appeal was allowed to stay on the land for her lifetime. She walked from Youghal to London wheeling her daughter in front of her, to beg the Queen for a pension and Raleigh gave her a present of an Azane cherry tree. She argued with William Shakespeare while he was presenting one of his plays in Youghal, telling him he was wrong to depict Richard III as a hunchback because she knew him personally and that he wasn't a hunchback and that he danced at her wedding. When the skeletal remains of King Richard were discovered in 2015 she was proved right. The bones showed that Richard had adolescent idiopathic scoliosis. This caused a slight curvature to the spine but would not have made him a hunchback. The legend also tells us that she grew three sets of teeth and she fell from a tree while picking cherries and died some time around the year 1604 when she was 140 years old or older.

There are several books that mention her life, some of which even question her life, so it is easy to demolish some of the myths. Richard Sainthill wrote *The Old Countess of Desmond: An Inquiry,* in 1861. Richard Sainthill says that the legal basis for her having the land dates back to 1464 and that – probably – people understood that the marriage or her birth occurred then. She might have been very happy to encourage that story and embellished it with details of life before she was even born – details about King Edward, about King Richard III and his hunchback condition. Such little gems of knowledge add verisimilitude to a good story. She may as a young person have spent some time in the London with the royal family and picked up stories.

Sainthill points out that the earliest she can have married is 1605, as her husband had another wife until then, which would make her over 40 years of age getting married, a very unlikely event. Sainthill demolishes some of the myths, while passionately believing that she was 'very olde, possibly even one hundred and four years old when he died'. She probably did not have three sets of teeth, her memory of Richard III is probably no more than a folk memory and her trip to London is probably confused with the trip of another Countess of Desmond – Eleanor – whose husband was in the Tower of London at the time.

Several portraits of the Olde Countess can be seen in Dromana House (open to visitors) where Katherine Fitzgerald was born. There is a most intriguing cabinet made from cherry wood after a tree was chopped down in the garden, some hundreds of years ago. Could it be the fateful tree that killed the countess?

It is hard to be precise about anything involving Katherine Fitz-gerald, as contemporary references are scanty. Walter Raleigh mentions her in his *History of the World* – he says, 'I myself knew the old Countess of Desmond, of Inchiquin, in Munster who lived in the year 1589, and many years since, who was married in Edward IV's time …'

There is a beautiful signet ring in the National Museum in Dublin which belonged to her. Inchiquin Castle can be visited, but is in a derelict condition.

RICHARD BOYLE

From the early 1600s onwards Boyle is the most significant person in the development of Youghal and other towns. He, and his family after him, continue to control the destiny, the fortunes and the development of Youghal for almost 400 years and they still own land and fishing rights in the area. His tomb in Youghal was considered to be outrageous, even scandalous, ostentatious and vulgar. It probably is, but there is a huge amount of history built into the tomb – his little stillborn child, the family marriages he arranged for his children, his incredible wealth and his two wives. It is a book in itself and the subject of many essays. Just in case he did not die in Youghal, he commissioned two more tombs. Many people regretted that he did not get to use one earlier. He died in Youghal in 1643, while the great Irish rebellion was underway. One of his sons was killed in that war, in the Battle of Liscannor, in which four of his sons fought.

Boyle arrived in Ireland in 1588 at the age of 22. He married a wealthy young woman, Joan Apsley who died in childbirth. He remarried, this time to Catherine Fenton, a few years later and his second wife bore him fifteen children. He was imprisoned many times for fraud, tax evasion and other charges, but was able to extricate himself from all difficulties. His political star rose and rose and he acquired several titles (Lord Cork, Baron Youghal, Sherrif of Youghal, Lord Justice and Lord Treasurer of Ireland.

An incredibly astute businessman, Boyle took the Raleigh lands and turned them into gold, earning more as a landlord than any other landlord in the British Isles. In 1613 the lands were earning him £4,000 (he only paid £1,500 for the estate) but this had increased by 1630 to £20,000, according to Professor Nicholas Canny. He spotted opportunities where others failed to do so. He thought Clonakilty would be a fine site for a town:

> For that is a most convenient place for a town, where I have already made a plantation of some hundred English families, that lying upon the sea-coast, where a ship of good burden may come up to the very town, and it will be the fittest place for a shire town when the Co. Corke, which is now over spacious for one shire shall be divided …

There was a suggestion going around for some time that Cork was too big and that it should be divided into two counties with one half being 'County Youghal'. This was suggested by the Youghal Town Council in 1584 but here one gets the distinct impression that the county town Boyle wanted was Clonakilty, not Youghal. The idea floated around for a while, but if the Boyles did not lend support, it was unlikely to succeed. The idea was last discussed in 1714.

In his study of Richard Boyle, Michael Twomey feels almost aggrieved that the modern-day people of Youghal promote the name of Raleigh rather than Boyle who, without any doubt, was far more significant in the development of the modern town. At one point Boyle had around 4,000 people working in his mines, iron foundries, shipping, tree felling and general estate management. His meticulous diaries are available online. One suspects that the name of Raleigh has greater iconic value, greater marketability than Boyle and purely on a personality level – Raleigh was a far more likeable rogue than Boyle. Nicholas Canny's study of Boyle is appropriately titled *The Upstart Earl*.

It is probably easier to agree with Professor Tadhg O'Keeffe that Raleigh straddles the two worlds, the old Gaelic and Anglo Norman world on one side and the brash new world of Boyle and his like on the other. Or you could agree with Dr Dagmar O'Riain-Raedel that history stops with Raleigh and everything after him is just journalism!

Boyle arranged the restoration of a part of St Mary's church, which is now referred to as the Boyle chapel, as it houses his tomb. He also made provision for veteran soldiers by building six alms houses. He built a school and left money to pay for a teacher. The fund survives to the present day, although the £5-a-year salary would not, on its own, attract many applicants!

He kept a firm hold on his lands, paid for hundreds of garrison troops out of his own money, and noted every detail which might be of use to him. This included every debt, every button, every lease of land, every present given.

A frequent visitor, who also borrowed money from him, was Sir Hardress Waller, who a few years later would be one of the men who signed the death warrant for King Charles I. Robert Phaire, another regicide, was one of Roger Boyle's officers. Phaire was one of the three colonels who arranged the execution of King Charles in 1649 on the instruction of Oliver Cromwell. An officer in Phaire's regiment was Valentine Greatrakes, whose later faith healing ability was closely and scientifically studied by Robert Boyle, another of his sons. Greatrakes featured in the witchcraft trial in Youghal.

Boyle had sixteen children – many of them very noteworthy figures. Robert Boyle is the best known of them because of the law in science named after him, but a number of the sons, feature in the story of Youghal, especially his son Broghill, whose hatred of Catholics was palpable. He had an astute political brain that enabled him to fight alongside Cromwell against King Charles I and later to be raised to the peerage by the restored monarch Charles II.

When Cromwell left Youghal to complete his conquest of Ireland, his army was divided into a three-pronged attack on the

Confederate forces, with one prong led by Broghill who hanged the Bishop of Macroom, Mac Egan on 11 May 1650 when the bishop refused to ask the soldiers to surrender. The second prong of the attack was led by Robert Phaire and the third by Cromwell himself.

Richard Boyle died in Youghal in 1643 and is buried in St Mary's collegiate church in what was described as the most ostentatiously vulgar tomb of its day. He was, by then, Earl of Cork and his colours (red and white) are still the county colours. He suffered substantial losses during the Great Rebellion but his sons more than recovered what he had lost.

Some years later the male line of the Boyles failed but the family, through marriage, continues to be involved in the estate:

Richard, 4th Earl of Cork and 3rd of Burlington, great grandson of the 1st Earl, died this year (1753) without male issue. His only child, Charlotte Elizabeth, had married the 28th March 1748, William, Marquis of Harrington, eldest son of William 3rd Duke of Devonshire, and she carried with her into the Cavendish family the barony of Clifford, with most of the Irish property of the Boyles, including Youghal.

THE SOCIETY OF FRIENDS/QUAKERS

Robert Sandham was, to use a Quaker expression, 'convinced' when he heard a Quaker called Elizabeth Fletcher preaching in the streets of Youghal. He became a Quaker. There were others who were equally convinced and a small but influential community developed in Youghal from the mid-1600s until the early 1900s. Sandham suffered for his new found beliefs which the Puritans attempted to destroy in an attempt to 'purify' their form of religion.

Quakers would not carry arms, would not accept important roles such as mayor or bailiff in the town, would not financially support the Protestant clergy and would not swear on a Bible. Sandham was imprisoned for refusing to swear an oath on the Bible, and his horse was confiscated. Roger Boyle set him free, as he saw no threat from the Quakers. His house was later the home of the Fisher family, the single most prolific and influential Quaker family in Youghal.

Edward Laundy was a very wealthy Quaker merchant. He coined his own money tokens and built a quay for his ships. He too was convinced by Elizabeth Fletcher. He went into St Mary's church where he began to preach to the Protestant congregation about the error of their ways. This did not go down well with the local Protestant population who did not appreciate being told of the error of their ways. According to Hayman, writing in the *Handbook for Youghal*, Laundy 'was very roughly handled ... was stoned and otherwise abused'.

Laundy's son, Jeremiah, married Martha Fisher. Quakers married Quakers if possible. Laundy is mentioned by William Penn who was happy with his meeting with him. However, Edward Laundy seems to have had an awkward relationship with the Quakers and does not feature in Richard S. Harrison's research into the Quakers. Perhaps it is because Laundy 'let the side down' – by accepting the office of Mayor of Youghal and, even worse, he offered to sponsor a horse race. Gaming of all kinds was strongly discouraged by the Quakers. Perhaps, to use a Youghal expression, 'he joined out'! Harrison corrected the omission in a paper to a Youghal Celebrates History Conference in 2015.

Other Quakers in the town were prominent merchants and many of the quays bear their name – including Grubb and Harvey.

THE HUGUENOTS IN YOUGHAL

In 1598 the Edict of Nantes guaranteed Protestants freedom of conscience, freedom of worship and civil liberties. In 1685 the Edict was revoked which led to a large number of Huguenots leaving France to find a more welcoming home. A number of them came to Youghal. From their titles (captain, cornet, ensign) it would seem that most of those who came to Youghal were military men who had served with Prince William of Orange. They easily fitted in to the ultra-Protestant environment in Youghal and within a generation were featured on civic lists. Joseph Labatte, for example, was mayor in 1751 and 1752, having previously served as bailiff.

In the course of time some of the names became anglicised – for example Dehays became Hays. Initially it was decided they could have voting rights on payment of sixpence but after a while the Corporation in Youghal was so happy with the Huguenots that it offered to fund the move of more Huguenots from France to the town, especially military men.

In some towns there was a separate church for Huguenots but not, it seems, in Youghal where Huguenot names are immediately seen among the births, marriages and deaths in St Mary's collegiate church.

WILLIAM CONGREVE (1670–1729)

William Congreve was born in England but the family relocated to Youghal in 1674, where his father served in the garrison and later took employment as an agent of the Duke of Devonshire. He went to school in Kilkenny where he met Jonathan Swift who became a lifelong friend. Swift even bought a house in Youghal.

He wrote several plays (*The Old Bachelor*, *The Mourning Bride*, *Love for Love*, and *The Way of the World*) and has given some memorable lines to the English language:

> 'Music has charms to soothe a savage breast'
> 'Hell hath no fury like a woman scorned'
> 'You must not kiss and tell.'
> 'Married in haste, repent at leisure'
> 'Never go to bed angry, stay up and fight!'

PIARAS MAC GEARAILT (FITZGERALD)

In 1759, the local poet Piaras Mac Gearailt, born near Youghal, with a very heavy heart 'went up the hill'. That is what he wrote in one of his poems. It meant he started to attend the Protestant church in Kilcredan in order to keep his land and keep his family together. Under English law all Catholics had to subdivide their land equally among their sons. The consequences of this law led to smaller and smaller farms and inevitably led to the Great Famine. A man has, say 100 acres and four sons. The second generation has twenty-five acres, the third generation about six acres so, for each generation, the farm gets smaller and the margin for survival gets tighter. The act was called the 'Act to prevent the further growth of Popery' and was passed into law in 1703. It was the single most unjust act passed by Parliament and led directly to the deaths of millions of people.

Any Catholic who changed religion could pass the farm to his eldest son and prevent the inevitable descent into poverty and starvation. Piaras Mac Gearailt, in name anyway, agreed to attend the Protestant church. He 'went up the hill'. His family farm remained intact.

He was a strong supporter of Bonny Prince Charlie as his 'Battle Song of Munster' tells:

> In storm or calm at peep of day
> With eager steps I seek the day
> And train my eyes and hope to see
> The first glimpse of our Prince's fleet.

Mac Gearailt's son, Michael, figured in the 1798 Rebellion as a member of the United Irishmen, so he retained his Jacobite loyalties.

SAMPSON TOWGOOD ROCH
(1757–1847)

Although born deaf and dumb Sampson Towgood Roch (or Roche) overcame severe disability to develop a major talent in art and has left an invaluable insight into rural life in Youghal with his sketchbooks as well as a series of miniature paintings of the rich and famous, including the royal family. He was, apparently, self-taught. His miniature paintings provided him with a thriving business. He received commissions from all sorts of people from the royal family to wealthy merchants and farmers.

After a successful career as a portrait artist in England, he returned to Ireland in 1822 to live in Wooodbine Hill near Youghal, where he began to sketch the local people and their occupations. He lived near the Ferry Point and probably often took the little ferry across to Youghal.

Many members of his family were prominent officers in the British forces over the various generations. Descendants today run a major entertainment business in the town. Most of the family is buried near the Round Tower in Ardmore.

There is some doubt about where Sampson Towgood Roch is buried – possibly in the unmarked space in the family plot in Ardmore. We do know he got married in St Mary's collegiate church where the minister added a comment about the dreadful affliction of being born deaf and dumb.

FR PETER O'NEILL

There is a fine statue in the Green Park in Youghal dedicated to the memory of Fr O'Neill and the events of 1798. Ever since the American War of Independence people all over Europe began to talk of democracy and republics. Events in France, which led to the execution of King Louis XVI, led to the formation of what was called the United Irishmen in this country and by 1795 they were planning to rebel against the English Government and hoping for French military help with their project. There was a rebellion in 1798 but it was limited to a few places. This is the story of what happened in Youghal.

The authorities were very aware of plans for a rebellion and took effective counteraction. Central to this action was the policy of 'Free Quarters'. The army would take over a large district and announce 'Free Quarters'. The locals had ten days to give up guns, pikes, weapons or soldiers would be instructed to go into houses to search. The soldier would also be able to take whatever food they wanted, to live in the house and to do whatever was necessary to get information about hidden weapons.

The policy of Free Quarters essentially terrorised people. Soldiers could take over people's houses as they went along, making free of the 'wives and wines' of their hosts. Soldiers were permitted to threaten and beat their host if he remonstrated. A family might have one cow, or one pig, or a few chickens – anything edible would be taken.

There was tension in the air in the run up to the rebellion and the army response was strong, severe and ruthless in subduing the population with appalling severity. In Youghal the Wexford militia were helping defend the town. They were very brutal. The troops wanted information any way they could get it. If the response was not satisfactory they began a campaign of absolute terror – pitch caps, maiming, half hanging, flogging, mutilation, killing of livestock. If weapons were found in a house it was to be set on fire and the occupants transported. As weapons were found they were displayed on the North Gate of Youghal.

There are stories of pitch caps – filling a cap with boiling tar and placing it on the head of a rebel. There were unofficial executions. One hanging was of a French soldier who refused to give his name – even when spoken to in French by one of the French Huguenots from the town. Another prisoner in the town jail, a man called Desmond, was hanged without trial along with his brother. The militia took a pole or spar from a ship and made a makeshift gallows by jamming the spar between two windows. Two members of the United Irishmen were found guilty and hanged from the windows of the Clock Gate. They were Charles Brien and Charles Gallagher.

In the list of trials in the National Archives in Dublin many of summary executions are not mentioned, although the trial of the local priest Fr Peter O'Neill is and the execution of his cousin.

In Ballymacoda, near Youghal, a man, called Patrick Murphy was murdered in December 1797. It was thought he was about to give information to the authorities about the activities of the United Irishmen in the area. Patrick Murphy was a weaver but also a member of the South Cork Militia. The killers secretly buried him. Some say he was buried near Fanisk, in a deep water hole, weighed down with stones, other accounts say he was buried at Knockadoon.

This was a major issue for the army – one of their own was murdered. It had to be the United Irishmen who did it but they didn't know who. They assumed Father O'Neill (the local parish priest) had to have known about it. In fact, they believed he approved of the murder. He was supposed to have been chairman of the group who organised it. He may even have given absolution before the crime was committed. Fr O'Neill was arrested and brought to the Clock Gate for interrogation and flogging to get a confession.

The rumour mill was in full swing. The flogging was an awful punishment – a whip usually had nine pieces of leather each with little knots. There were rules about how many lashes could be given, but in times of trouble such as 1798, such niceties went out the window and hundreds of lashes, in some cases a thousand lashes or even fifteen-hundred lashes were given. Every now and then they would stop to make sure the prisoner would not die. And then more lashes, more screaming. The ground around the whipping post was stained red. The awful shrieks of agony echoed all over the town. It was said they were 'whipped to within an inch of their life'.

Three people in total were arrested for the murder – Fr Peter O'Neill, Thomas O'Neill and Michael Fitzgerald. Philip O'Nell has a fine book on the episode. Under interrogation Fr O'Neill is said to have confessed everything. This is most unlikely as a confession would certainly have led to his immediate execution. He received some 300 lashes before being tried and transported. Having served his sentence he returned to Ireland and is buried in Ballymacoda.

Of the other two arrested for the murder, Thomas O'Neill was brought to Cork and hanged on the Grand Parade. While Micheal Fitzgerald was found to be not guilty (he was the son of the poet Piaras Mac Gearailt).

Inside the town it was found that blacksmiths were making pikes for the United Irishmen. One blacksmith, Padrageen na Gow (or little Paddy the blacksmith) was flogged. He did not confess. He actually boasted the flogging cured his asthma.

In total, after the raids and punishments 1,174 pikes were discovered or handed in.

In 1799 the Corporation of Youghal noted in its records 'the late unhappy distractions', possibly referring to the reign of terror imposed by the army in Youghal, the imposing of Free Quarters, murders, floggings, mutilations and transportations. Yes, indeed, they were unhappy distractions. The Lord Lieutenant of Ireland congratulated the town council on forming their own Yeomanry, possibly just in case any more 'unhappy distractions' might occur and they, in turn, promised eternal loyalty to him.

FATHER DANIEL KELLER (1839–1922)

Irish Catholic tenants began to campaign for certain 'rights' after the Irish Famine of the 1840s. These rights became known as the 'Three Fs' – meaning Fair Rent, Fixity of Tenure and Free Sale. Essentially tenants were looking for a lease at a reasonable rent and the right to sell that lease. This was a right that Protestant tenants had but not Catholics. In the 1880s there was a series of bad summers and poor harvests. Many tenants could not pay their rent.

The 'Plan of Campaign' as it was called involved asking landlords to reduce their rent in the light of the dire economic circumstances of the tenants. They would offer the landlord a reduced rent. If the landlord refused, the rent would be paid into a bank account held by a trusted member of the community. In the case of Youghal the tenants on the Ponsonby estate adopted the plan in 1886. The landlord was offered the rent, less 35 per cent. This was refused. The tenants then paid the money to a trustee. This was widely believed to be the local parish priest, Fr Daniel Keller who was known to be a strong supporter of tenant rights and had shared a platform with Charles Stuart Parnell.

Keller had a brilliant mind, a former professor of philosophy in Paris, who returned to Ireland to take a post as curate in Cobh and became parish priest of Youghal in 1885.

Ponsonby began to evict tenants, first individually and later in larger numbers. The evicted tenants erected tents at the old Ardagh church outside Youghal. The weather in 1887 grew bitterly cold and there were many deaths.

Fr Keller was summoned to Dublin in 1887 to answer the charge that he was the trustee of the account. He failed to appear and a warrant was issued for his arrest by Judge Boyd. There was widespread consternation in Youghal where the people began to protest. Crowds and marching bands took to the streets. Some of the men ominously carried tar barrels (a reminder of a traditional form of punishment). The windows in the police barracks were broken. District Inspector Kerins's home was attacked. A group of women attacked the bailiff and beat him severely. Shops were boarded up. Reinforcements arrived by train. The army and police fixed bayonets and charged the protesters. One local man, Patrick

Supplement Gratis with "UNITED IRELAND." Saturday March 26th 1887

THE CONSECRATION OF KILMAINHAM JAIL.

THE TWO ARCHBISHOPS bless Father Keller and his Cross

Hanlon from Ballymacoda, was killed. The bishop sent a letter to Fr O'Neill asking him to 'do the necessary' to prevent further bloodshed.

Fr Keller surrendered himself to the authorities and was sentenced to jail by Judge Boyd. He was triumphantly escorted to Kilmainham Jail by the Archbishop of Dublin and crowds of well-wishers. He remained in jail for two months. He was promoted to canon during his imprisonment.

There was an inquest on the death of Patrick Hanlon. The coroner issued a verdict of wilful murder. Both the chief constable of police and the actual policeman who did the killing were charged with murder but subsequently acquitted by the court. The people of Ballymacoda erected a special memorial to the memory of Patrick Hanlon. That ceremony was attended by over 3,000 people.

Canon Keller was eventually freed when the court found that he was not obliged by law to divulge whether or not he had access to the tenants' money. He returned a hero and there were major celebrations in Youghal. Keller wrote a book *The Struggle for Life on the Ponsonby Estate*, a struggle which on the Ponsonby estate and other estates around Youghal got steadily worse. More public meetings were organised.

In March 1888, William O'Brien, Member of Parliament and supporter of Parnell held a meeting at the Mall House in Youghal. He tried to have the meeting in the Green Park, but the army and police prevented it. Special trains were used to bring troops quickly to Youghal, to ensure law and order and prevent access to the Green Park. Militants ripped up the railway tracks and broke telegraph wires to delay the army's activities. The tenants got more and more angry. Houses were being fortified strongly against the military and police. In many cases the army and police noted the resolve of the owners and quietly went away for reinforcements.

On the Ponsonby estate things went from bad to worse. Ponsonby sold his estate to a consortium from London who were determined to break the power of the tenants. The remaining 400 were to be evicted in four separate groups if they did not pay the required rent. In June 1889 and April, September and October 1890, with the cooperation of the army, all the designated houses except for 100 were broken down and the tenants evicted. In 1892 the remaining 100 tenants accepted the terms on offer and returned to their homes. Canon Keller continued his steadfast support for the tenants.

In his twilight years Canon Keller could not understand the suffragette movement, led by Anna Haslam from Youghal, and at an address to the local Loreto girls and their parents he asked

'Who are these suffregettes?' He answered his question with a little witticism which was widely reported in the national newspapers …

> Who are these suffragettes? They are NOT, in my opinion, LADIES, as I understand the term (Hear! Hear!) and they certainly are not MEN
> (loud guffaws from male parents)
> They must be what the French call 'A Third Sex'
> (loud applause from all, cries of 'Hear Hear etc.).

He is buried in front of St Mary's Catholic church in Youghal.

ISAAC BUTT

Butt served as MP for Youghal from 1852 to 1865. He was a well-known barrister who had serious financial difficulties during his life. This led to him serving any cause that would pay him. He defended the Young Irelanders who were on trial after the failed uprising of 1848 but also served the Duke of Devonshire in defending his fishing rights on the River Blackwater and later again defended the Fenians after their attempted uprising. The Duke of Devonshire paid him an annual retainer, which was always welcome, as Butt had major debts.

Election days were very tense with supporters of the candidates openly aggressive and intimidating towards perceived opponents and their supporters. On 14 July 1852 the 72nd Highland Regiment were supported by the 90th Light Infantry and the 7th Dragoon Guards to ensure order on the streets during that year's election. Butt won by two votes.

During his time as Member of Parliament he founded the Home Rule League, which became a major issue for Irish people for the next forty years.

Butt had a certain weakness for hard drink and sex, which led to him fathering several children, and earned him a spell in the Debtor's Prison as he had multiple debts which he never managed to fully resolve.

DAVID LEOPOLD LEWIS

In 1861 the people of Youghal welcomed Lewis with open arms, as did Youghal Town Council and various other illustrious people, including the Duke of Devonshire. He was behind the newly-reconstituted Cork and Youghal Railway line. Some thought he was the owner. There was a public meeting to welcome him to town and to wish him well in his new home at The College, former home of Richard Boyle, first Earl of Cork. He more or less bought the town of Youghal by buying the Duke of Devonshire's leases and rent books. Hundreds of houses and entire streets all became the property of the amazing financial wizard David Leopold Lewis, the new 'saviour' of the town.

He had, he said to the Town Council, major plans for Youghal. These were recorded in the *Cork Examiner*, which included in this report the reaction of the Town Council. He had commissioned the artist Stopford to undertake a series of sketches which would show the world that the 'Irish Rhine' was as wonderful as the real thing. *(Cries of 'Hear! Hear!' from council members.)*

Lewis was certain that Youghal would become a wonderful tourist resort. He would arrange trains from Cork to Youghal and passengers could then board specially commissioned paddle steamers to take them to Cappoquin and back! There would be trains when Youghal Fair was being held. There would be regattas and he would provide special trains to bring spectators from far and wide. Youghal would become a seaside resort for day trips, for longer excursions and for holidays. He would put Youghal on the map. *(Further widespread applause.)*

He had plans for a whole series of houses to be built near the railway station – beautiful summer homes for the people who would, undoubtedly, begin to grace the wonderful seaside resort of Youghal and the new suburb of Lewisville would have highly sought houses in the splendid Victorian Gothic style, they would become much sought-after architectural gems. *(Hear! Hear!)*

(Lewis forgot to mention that this would involve evicting the existing tenants – a minor detail.)

He had plans for the town council on improving the town, on turning it into a nationally known resort. Even internationally known! *(Widespread applause.)*

Youghal would be the 'Brighton of Ireland' and the River Black-water would be the Irish Rhine! (*Thunderous applause.*)

The townspeople were delighted. Here was a man who would save the town. That year the benevolent man gave 100 tons of coal to needy families as well as blankets. The town began to buzz with excitement. Advertisements in the local *Examiner* were offering the kinds of excursions he spoke of with special fares for first, second and third class passengers. Everyone could afford it! First a train journey then a cruise up the majestic Blackwater. What a wonderful idea!

Unfortunately, the fairy tale did not last. Lewis forgot to mention he had been in jail in Lancaster in 1852 for debt and, on his release, was re-arrested some months later, again for debt. In 1855 he was trying to pawn plate and jewels but then he had a better idea. He moved to Ireland and became the financial adviser to the newly-formed Cork and Youghal Railway. In fact, he bought substantial shares in the company and offered security for the purchase. The security he offered was taken at face value and no questions were asked.

He negotiated a sale of bonds to raise half a million pounds in shares but it needed parliamentary approval. The House of Commons sanctioned the company the ability to raise the half a million pounds in bonds to finance its activities. Lewis, perhaps by genuine error, raised twice that amount but, when the bonds were called in, the funds were not there. Nor were there assets for his own purchases. Enquiries were made and alarming discoveries made about the true financial situation of David Leopold Lewis. The railway company now had debts of almost a million pounds without the means to pay. The House of Commons wound up the company and Lewis was again declared a bankrupt.

The houses in Lewisville remain architectural gems, just as he predicted, but most of his other plans, and David Leopold Lewis himself, slipped quietly away. He died in 1867 leaving lawyers work for several years. However, his plans were at least ambitious even if ultimately ending in abject failure.

THE HORGAN BROTHERS

One of the most talented families in Youghal during the late nineteenth and all of the twentieth century was the Horgan family.

Many of them died during the Great Famine but, one of them, Ted Horgan survived, just about, and his three sons made a gigantic contribution to the history of Youghal with their inventiveness and business acumen.

The three sons were Thomas, Jim and Philip. Tom was more involved in experimentation, while Jim was the more artistic of the three, but all three shared the work. Tom saw a camera for sale in Merrick's stores and was immediately captivated at the thought of what it might do. He bought the camera and quickly learned how to develop the glass-plate negatives. In those early days they had great fun figuring out the way negative images might turn out ... Would left be right? Was up down? But they quickly mastered the technique.

The three boys soon opened their own shop. One half of their shop sold shoes, the other half became a photographic studio and depending on the customer, the boys would appear with a shoemaker's leather apron or a white coat more appropriate to the photography business. There was a great demand for boots among the army officers in town but there was an even greater demand for photographs. The studio became more and more elaborate, with backdrops, costumes and various props, which led to a great sense of fun for those having their photographs taken.

They realised there was an enormous demand for photographs – weddings, family photographs, emigration, wakes, religious processions, events in the town. That led to other possibilities such as postcards. This led to long hours in the dark room, up to fourteen hours a day, developing the images to keep up with the ever-increasing demand for photographs. A regular input in the *Cork Weekly Examiner* began in the early 1900s. This is particularly helpful today as many photographs were undated at that time.

They learned about limelight and how to burn it to create a bright light to project images on to walls. They began to travel to towns around Youghal to take photographs and to display them using the 'magic lantern' and an ingenious 3D type system using twin images of the same item so that both eyes were used separately, creating thereby a 'third image'.

Jim began to experiment with touching up photos, adding tinges of colour while Tom became adept at blending two images together to create new scenes. There is a famous image of the Clock Gate looking as if it is a bridge over a river, as if Youghal was Venice. They began to animate images and there is an amazing little animated film showing the Clock Gate doing cartwheels and waltzing around before dancing over to Ardmore.

The Lumière Brothers had begun to make motion pictures but were reluctant to share the technology. Their projection equipment could be bought and short films they had made were available. The Horgans modified the equipment to make their own camera. In particular they wanted to film the arrival of King Edward at Lismore. Local police were very wary of the three brothers with their large 'contraption',which might have concealed a weapon. Fortunately the king had seen moving picture cameras and stopped to doff his hat to the Horgans, while the queen waved. A priceless piece of film was the result of their vision.

However, it was not just national type news for which we are grateful to the Horgans. They also filmed local events, local people doing ordinary things – like going in and out of church. After a visit from Henry Ford, who wanted his picture taken, they accepted his advice that the cinema was the next big thing. There was a huge concern about the safety of gases used in projection, so custom-built cinemas were necessary.

The brothers built their own cinema and, in addition to outside films, also showed a *Youghal Gazette*, a compilation of local news, which was guaranteed to fill the house. Today the *Youghal Gazette* is a major source of local history, much like the local Community Radio Youghal.

Jim Horgan painted the walls of his business premises with local scenes. Unfortunately the paintings were hacked off the walls by a later purchaser. The house they lived in served as a testing place for Jim's artwork and the entire front room, hallway and staircase retain full-size paintings of what was later in the cinema.

In the early days of silent films the brothers and other members of the family made up the orchestra that played the accompanying music, as many of them were gifted musicians (or married to musicians).

The cinema itself features in stories by writers like William Trevor (*Memories of Youghal*) and in the folklore of the town. The cinemea lasted right up to the 1960s.

Today over 700 of the Horgan images are preserved in the Cork County Archives, and extracts from their film work can be seen

104, NORTH MAIN STREET, YOUGHAL.

HORGAN'S PICTURE THEATRE
YOUGHAL

Each Evening at 8.30.   Matinees : Sunday, 3.30 ; Wednesday, 3.45.

WEEK COMMENCING SATURDAY, JANUARY 4, 1947.

Saturday, Sunday and Monday—

ALAN LADD and GAIL RUSSELL in

" SALTY O'ROURKE "

With William Demarest, Stanley Clements, Bruce Cabot, Spring Byington, etc. An exciting story of the race track coupled with a heart-warming romance. The king of films about the sport of kings.
ALSO FULL SUPPORTING PROGRAMME.

Tuesday and Wednesday—

JEAN HERSHOLT and DOROTHY LOVETT in

" COURAGEOUS DR. CHRISTIAN "

With a strong supporting cast. A delightful addition to this popular series. A story that will appeal to all.
ALSO FULL SUPPORTING PROGRAMME.

Thursday and Friday—

ALAN MARSHAL and LARAINE DAY in

" BRIDE BY MISTAKE "

With Marsha Hunt, Allyn Joslyn, Edgar Buchanan, Marc Cramer, Nancy Gates, etc. A super comedy romance with many hilarious situations and sparkling love interest. A story of love versus money.
Also GEORGE SANDERS and WENDY BARRIE in

" A DATE WITH THE FALCON "

With James Gleason, Allen Jenkins, Mona Maris, Victor Kilian, etc. Comedy, romance and thrills blended in an exciting detective story. One of the best of this popular series.

COMING : "THE STORY OF G. I. JOE," "DANGEROUS PASSAGE," "ABOVE SUSPICION," "BRING ON THE GIRLS," "ON BORROWED TIME," "RAGE IN HEAVEN," "PRINCESS AND THE PIRATE," ETC.

on YouTube as the family has graciously made most of their work available to the public. Stories of the major events in Youghal can be enjoyed as pictures, which, as always are worth a thousand words.

OUR LADY OF GRACES

In various locations around Youghal there are images of the Madonna holding a child. There is a prominent one where the road forks to facilitate one-way traffic into town from the Cork side, one in The College gardens and one in the North Abbey grounds. There are a number of legends attached to the Madonna image and devotion to it persists to the present day, both in Youghal and Cork where the image is presently housed. The image is of carved ivory, very worn and housed in a specially made case with the name Honora Fitzgerald inscribed on it.

In 1268 the Dominican monks came to Youghal and set up an abbey, which is now called the North Abbey. Most of the abbey is gone, but a few pillars remain, giving some idea of the scale of the building.

There are two main stories about the origin of the statue. In one version, a log floated in on the tide. Local fishermen could not lift it but two monks hoisted it on their shoulders easily and brought it to the porch of the church. A blind man fumbling for holy water touched the wet wood and blessed himself. Suddenly he could see. The Dominican prior had a dream that there was something inside the log. There was. Inside the log of wood was a tiny statue of the Madonna and child. The story spread quickly and soon thousands were visiting the church to see the miraculous statue. Youghal became a place of pilgrimage, until Sir Walter Raleigh ordered that the church be demolished.

In the second version of the story the Archbishop of Cashel, Maurice O'Carroll (who served from 1303 to 1316) while on a visit to Youghal became very sick and died. He asked that his image of the Madonna and child, which he always wore on his body, be buried with him. It was. The Dominican Prior had a dream that the statue should not be lost to the public and had the coffin dug up and the little image was put on display. Samuel Hayman doubted both stories, as he believed the statue to have been made in Italy in the middle of the fifteenth century. Either way the two main stories have strong similarities, and one could trust the Church authorities not to leave a potential gold mine disappear forever.

In 1586 Sir Walter Raleigh became the new owner of the church and, a year later, ordered that it be knocked down. To make sure it would not be rebuilt, the stones were transported to the grounds of The College, were they form the core of the external wall of the gardens. Sections of pillars and windows can be seen in the wall.

The statue was rescued and given to Honora Fitzgerald who had a special case made for it. It was kept for a long time in the Fitzgerald castle at Ballymaloe, before eventually finding its way to the Dominican church of St Mary's in Pope's Quay, Cork. A beautiful shrine was made for the statue and it is still there.

YOUGHAL LACE

The ladies of Belfast decided to make a presentation to Queen Alexandra in honour of her coronation of a train of lace, and commissioned the ladies of Youghal to make it. The work was undertaken by the nuns of the Presentation Convent who had revived the lacemaking tradition back in the days of the Famine and continued to train young girls in how to make lace.

They had three months to make the product, meaning the sixty-strong workforce had to work over 100 hours per week each to ensure it was completed on time. The stitches were difficult and complicated, requiring high levels of concentration over a sustained time – and electricity was not available! They couldn't afford to fall behind as the coronation deadline simply had to be met.

The nuns and sixty skilled lacemakers worked a total of 98,020 hours by day and night to finish the court train. It would have taken a single worker almost forty-nine years to do the same, assuming a forty-hour week!

It was considered by experts to be the 'most magnificent example of Irish needlepoint lace ever seen'. The design involved fuchsias, wild roses with scrolls of ribbon work, hawthorn and May flowers.

It has to be seen to be believed. The finished product is in London, in the Victoria and Albert Museum.

There was one small problem with the product after the 98,020 hours of work. In tiny detail the words '*deanta in Eirinn*' were included (meaning 'made in Ireland'). The ladies from Belfast insisted that these letters be removed before payment could be made!

ANNA HASLAM (*NÉE*) FISHER (1820–1922)

Anna Fisher was born in 1820 in Youghal, into one of the most prominent Quaker families in the town.

Perhaps one of the proudest moments in her life happened in December 1918, when, at the head of a large throng of triumphant women she went, for the first time in her life, to cast her vote. Sadly, her husband Thomas was not there to see the triumph, but the work of the couple is commemorated in St Stephen's Green in Dublin, where a garden bench is dedicated to their memory.

She was still in Youghal when the Great Famine began to affect the town. She worked in the soup kitchen organised by the Quakers and is credited with the idea of teaching lace as a means of providing women with a trade and an income. She taught some nuns how to make lace and they were astute learners who picked and unpicked the lace until they understood it perfectly and then began classes, thereby starting a business, which survives to the present day.

She married Thomas Haslam in 1854 and the couple moved to Dublin. She campaigned for the rest of her life about all sorts for human rights, especially the right of women to vote. There was considerable opposition to women being allowed to vote, as men believed that women could not endure the roughness and brutality of the polling booths. Well-meaning men also would not allow married women to own their own property, believing it to be too much for the little ladies to be bothered about. Others believed that women were too delicate in nature to benefit from a university education.

Anna Haslam was not deterred by such hogwash. In 1876 she founded the Women's Suffrage Association and in this work she was strongly supported by her husband. She wrote letter after letter to the newspapers about the need to include women. She saw the way the media could be used to spread her message.

She believed that the workhouses would be better managed if women were allowed on their boards of guardians. She asked women to put themselves forward for such positions. Men were flabbergasted that women would even want to take on such responsibilities. It was unheard of – but there was nothing actually forbidding it.

The Women's Enfranchisement Bill was defeated in 1905 but Anna Haslam continued to fight. She did not agree with the militants who were much more assertive in their demands. One woman threw a hatchet at Prime Minister Asquith when he visited Ireland in 1912.

In 1907 she formed groups of women to patrol the streets, to discourage immorality, begging and street trading. She invited women to involve themselves in court cases affecting women and children. She encouraged women to take up jury duty, arguing that in cases involving women, it would help considerably to have a woman's perspective on the case.

Reluctantly the authorities gave way. First married women were allowed to own property in their own right in 1882, and they were allowed to vote in local elections in 1891. Then women over 30, women who were university graduates, women who were householders or married to one were granted the right to vote in parliamentary elections and, after a long struggle, eventually universal suffrage was extended to all women in 1920 in Ireland, some eight years before women in England enjoyed the same privileges.

YOUGHAL CELEBRATES HISTORY

In 2003 a committee was formed to celebrate the history of Youghal and began to organise an annual conference, field trip and other events. Initially the town, in conjunction with University College Cork (UCC), formed a committee to celebrate the finding of a document in a German university. The document was a piece of Canon Law, one of the oldest manuscripts of its type. It had been transcribed in Molana Abbey, near Youghal.

An academic from UCC, Dr Dagmar O'Riain-Raedel, was the central driving force in organising a conference to celebrate the event. She was easily persuaded to examine other aspects of the town's history and to organise further conferences, which since 2003 have become a yearly event.

A list of the topics covered and the presenters who contribute to the various conferences gives an insight into the history of the town. Items such as the maritime tradition, the Fitzgeralds of Desmond, the life and times of Sir Walter Raleigh, Sir Richard Boyle, churches and cloisters, Youghal as a port in the eighteenth and nineteenth centuries, the medieval walled towns, politics and culture in the nineteenth century, tales from the tombs of St Mary's collegiate church, the armorial heritage, the trial for witchcraft of Florence Newton, Irish whiskey, the Quakers and the great houses. In addition to broad themes there are also papers on prominent families and individuals – such as the Cockburns, Edward Fitzgerald (the antiquarian), Samuel Hayman, Fr O'Neill and Fr Keller.

The group's activities can be seen on their website, with abstracts of presentations available. Many of the presenters have published their works, the most notable of these publications being the

Historic Town Atlas of Youghal, one of the series from the Royal Irish Academy. One of the co-authors, David Kelly, is a founder member of the group.

THE OLD PRINTING PRESS – LINDSAY/FIELD

There have been numerous publications celebrating the history of Youghal, and what is astonishing is that since 1824 many of them have been printed on the same printing press, still running in the same shop in North Main Street. The letters are faded in some cases but most people accept that old age does bring some extra burden on the lettering.

The printing press itself has much history attached to it. John Lindsay purchased a second-hand printing press in Cork in 1824. It had previously been owned by James Blow, a Belfast printer who claimed it was the very press on which the first Bible was printed in Ireland in 1704. John Lindsay died around 1850 in the workhouse in Youghal but his cousin, married to a man called Field, took over the business, which still survives.

Much, if not most, of the printed matter for Youghal was struck there – including concert programmes, cinema advertising, booklets, posters and postcards. These items, using the original press, can be bought in the same shop, sold by a member of the same Field family. Especially popular is a reproduction of Canon Hayman's *Handbook for Youghal,* usually the 1896 Lindsay edition and another popular item is the cinema poster for the first Youghal screening of the film *Moby Dick*.

HISTORIANS

Quite a number of people have told the story of Youghal, many of them from Youghal, and others who have come to love the town. There are several to discover – Samuel Hayman, Edward Fitzgerald, Maurice Fitzgerald, Thomas Cooke, Pierce Drew, Niall O'Brien, Claude Cockburn, Michael Hackett (sixty books on the history of Youghal), Frank Keane, Tom Fitgerald, Alicia

St Leger, David Kelly, Tadhg O'Keeffe, Ollie Casey, Michael Twomey and, literally, hundreds who have contributed research articles to various journals and scholarly books, including people like Clodagh Tait and Richard Harrison. They are all part of a long list.

Two lesser-known people were Mary Aher and William French who, individually, contributed a weekly column on local history over many years to the *Youghal Tribune*, especially the years 1940 to 1954. The *Tribune* tried to focus attention on history and the potential of the rich heritage of the town.

The *Tribune* reported on visits by historical societies, such as the Royal Society of Antiquaries who visited Youghal in May 1953 and the Midleton Historical and Archaeological Society who visited in 1947. 'Wake Up Youghal!' the *Tribune* screamed and begged people to realise the potential for the tourism business.

The *Tribune* no longer exists, but local history is still being well covered by the *East Cork News*, the *Youghal News*, Community Radio Youghal and other news media.

SAMUEL HAYMAN (1818–1886)

Hayman is mentioned several times in this book. He is often referred to as the 'Historian of Youghal'. His output was prodigious and numerous articles and books survive, especially the *Handbook for Youghal* (printed by W.G. Field in 1896). He also published several other booklets like the *Memorials of Youghal, Ecclesiastical and Civil* in 1879 which included the account of the visit by Thomas Dinely to Youghal in the year 1681 and several of Dinely's drawings of the town, printed by the same printing press.

Hayman probably could not avoid being interested in history. He was born in South Abbey, Youghal, to a family which came from Somerset, some time in the mid-1600s. An ancestor, Samuel Hayman, served as bailiff of Youghal in 1666 and mayor, for the first time, in 1670.

Another, Samuel Hayman was mayor in 1741. Atkin Hayman, the son of Samuel, was a minister at St Mary's in 1764, and invited John Wesley to preach there in 1765.

Wesley comments, in his *Journal*, on the ruinous state of part of the church: 'I was glad to see a large and tolerably serious congregation in the Church. It was once a spacious building; but more than half of it now (a common occurrence in Ireland) lies in ruins'.

Atkin Hayman's great-grandson was Matthew Hayman father of Samuel, the historian of whom we speak. He was appointed to St Mary's in 1849. He took a keen interest in the renovations of the church – and comments on the work, mentioning such observations as 'tastelessly converted' and 'well restored'.

Hayman is buried in Douglas, Cork city, but his contribution to the history of Youghal remains forever.

3

YOUGHAL THROUGH
THE AGES

Much of the old town retains the shape of the town depicted in the Pacata Hibernia map (p.54) that was made in the late seventeenth century. A large stretch of the town walls remain and the main street, divided into North and South Main Street is still as it was. Some of the little towers on the town walls remain. A few of the medieval lanes are still there, like Meatshambles Lane, Chapel Lane and North Cross Lane. The North and South division of Main Street begin at the Clock Gate. The beautiful College Gardens and Collegiate Church of St Mary are shown in the top right-hand corner of the map.

Some of the older buildings can still be discerned in the walls of newer buildings of Youghal. If, for example, the top of the castle was removed and the building converted into a private house, the building would still retain the thick walls of the castle. It is a town that slowly reveals its secrets. In one street there are buildings from the thirteenth to the twentieth century, side by side.

Entry to a town like Youghal was invariably via a gate – a land gate or a water gate. One of the water gates survives. In the map it is in the little docking area where there is a ship. This is where cargo was loaded and unloaded. It was from there that Oliver Cromwell left Youghal to return to Bristol. Sometimes that Watergate is called Cromwell's Arch.

Lots of different types of ships served the little port. There was initially the Viking long boat. It was easy to drag up on strands and beaches. There was a cargo-carrying version of this boat called a 'knarr'. By early medieval times the long boat was replaced by the 'cog' which was used for a variety of purposes. It could have had turrets front and rear for military use. It was flat bottomed which made it easy to load and unload on both river and sea sides. A development of the 'cog' was the 'hulk', which was curved to the front and rear. Both had a main sail in the centre of the boat.

The coat of arms of Youghal displays one of these early boats, with her mast in the centre. As boat building developed, a mast was designed more to the front of the vessel, which gave greater speed.

In medieval times Youghal was trading with towns in Italy, France and Portugal as well as England. Hides, cloth, fish and timber were the main exports at that stage with wine, oil, spices, salt and iron being imported.

By the seventeenth century the boats were getting bigger and bigger. Richard Boyle used a boat called a 'lighter' to transport the timber he cut from forests along the River Blackwater. In 1628 he transported 18,000 tons of timber in these 'lighters'. It would have taken at least 1,300 trips downriver to carry all the timber that year alone!

A few years after the map was made much of the seafront of the town was converted into quays. There was a substantial sea trade in and out of the town. However, a series of laws passed in England began to have a serious effect on any Irish trade, which might have competed with English trade. The demand for cattle and wood continued but heavy duties on Irish imports to England left Irish trade in an unhealthy place according to the historian Ruth Dudley Edwards.

As always, the Duke of Devonshire claimed ownership of the strand at the north end of the town from high water mark to the low water mark. On an anecdotal level, the claim came back to haunt the duke during the Great Famine, as the Board of Works decided to construct a big slob bank (which still exists) but insisted that the duke pay for it as he claimed the land was his. In fairness to him he did pay, with the starving people of Youghal providing the labour.

The town had one long street and a square, in the middle of which was a large crucifix. In the square, around the crucifix the town crier would shout out the news, beginning with the immortal words 'Oyez! Oyez' or 'Hear ye!' in English. In that square too would gather the casual merchants and traders selling their goods, going from town to town. From the council records we know what was being traded. In 1358 it was corn, malt, meal, salt, bark, coal, lime, all kinds of farm animals, fish, honey, onions, garlic, hinges, linen and silk, flax, leather, ale and wine, brass and copper and lots of other knickknacks and gewgaws. It is easy to imagine the street traders shouting their wares and busy town officials making sure that the tax was paid on each item.

Later the officials would become anxious about precise measurements for beer and spirits, for tobacco and foodstuffs and they tried to prevent the illegal undercutting of prices.

UNDER SIEGE

In 1579 the town was attacked and ransacked by the forces of the Earl of Desmond. This was part of the Munster Rebellion, which was crushed and led to the end of the Fitzgerald rule and the subsequent planation by English colonists.

> The Earl of Desmond and his forces encamped before Youghal, and finally took that town which, at that time, was full of riches and goods, excepting such gold and silver as the merchants and burgesses had sent away in ships before the town was taken … The Geraldines levelled the wall of the town and broke down its courts and castles, and its buildings of stone and wood; so that it was not habitable for some time afterwards.

LIFE IN TOWN

From the Council Book of Youghal there is a fascinating insight into the life of the town in the seventeenth century. The council were elected and very conscious of their position. They insisted they would be appropriately dressed (at their own cost): 'that all that be Aldermen and of the Council … shall at their own cost be provided with gowns befitting their degree, to wear as they accompany the Mayor.'

Having permission to buy and sell was very important as the council tried to fix prices and standards. It became a condition of becoming a freeman of the town that one agreed to the rules for buying and selling. This allowed the council to control the markets, demand taxes on all goods and pay the necessary taxes to the Crown.

> Edmund Brien was charged with buying wheat without permission and baking bread.
>
> Will Cornishe bought coal at 4 pennies a load and sold them for six pennies a load.
>
> Gerald FitzRichard built a ditch on the Kilcoran road without permission.

There were holes in the walls and many people were robbed by 'ill-disposed persons' who were able to slip in and out of town. The council ordered that the holes be filled with lime.

In 1616 a street cleaner was appointed to 'scavenge' the street and 'carry away the filth of every house as well as in lanes as in Broad Street, twice a week, viz, on Wednesdays and Saturdays ...'

Every family was to pay six pennies a year for the street cleaner's service and failure to pay would invoke a fine of twelve pennies. Between all the animals (horses, pigs, dogs and cows) there would be a lot to clean up. There was a problem with pigs roaming freely around the streets.

Provision was made a for a 'rapid response fire service'. This involved placing ladders and leather buckets, grappling irons and hooks near the town hall. Thatched houses would be banned within the town walls. The buckets were to have the arms of the town on them.

A constable was to go around town to see if people were not attending church and to punish them or report them. He was also to check taverns and alehouses to ensure they were closed and imprison any persons found on the premises after hours.

At eight o'clock at night a drummer would go around beating his drum, which would mean the nightwatch was being called upon to take up their duty. In 1618 it was Corneilius Lorgan who was the drummer and he had been for many years at an annual salary of twenty shillings.

There was a bit of controversy with the local schoolteacher Ulick Burke after he had retired but failed to leave the house he was living in. He was asked to surrender his lease to the land but that he would get it back on condition that he actually paid the rent of five pounds a year. The council would meanwhile seek to employ another teacher at four pounds a year: 'to teach the petty scholars and make them fit for the free-school.'

Security was very important and: 'every householder should, before Midsummer next, provide sufficient weapon for setting forth one man for the strength of the town, to have a sword by his side, a musket upon his shoulder, along with powder and bullets.

Following a visit from a visiting theatre company, there was found to be considerable damage to the Tholsel House by patrons. A glazier was appointed to fix the damage. Shakespeare was very popular in Youghal and a lot of people were trying to get in!

The council discussed the proclamation of 1621 by the Lord Deputy who expressly outlawed the practice of families sending sons abroad to further their education who would invariably return: 'corrupted in their religion and towards his Majesty and the present Government'.

The Lord Deputy demanded the return of all those young men studying abroad and failure to comply would result in fines, confiscation of goods and other measures. Mostly it was Catholic young men who went abroad for their education. This practice continued until the nineteenth century, when laws against Catholic education were relaxed.

The council ordered that an alms house or hospital be built next to the north side of the quay and that Sir Laurence Parsons would give ten pounds towards the construction. For those who broke the law there were punishments.

PUNISHMENTS

In the square near the cross, there was a cage for bold boys and, a 'cucking stool' for women, both set up in 1653. A woman who needed to be punished for some reason or other would be tied into the 'cucking stool' or chair. A woman might be punished for being a 'scold' – which meant she might be an angry nagging woman.

Or she may have been incontinent – which had a different meaning then, meaning a person unable to control their passions.

There was a 'bridle' in some towns, which involved a sort of cage around the woman's head and a metal bar forced into her mouth. In Youghal they used the 'cucking stool'. The word 'cucking' refers to an old Scandinavian word for excrement, suggesting perhaps that the punishment might loosen the bowels which would increase the humiliation for the woman tied to the chair or that the chair might sit in a pile of excrement. Punishments were public, humiliating events, meant to be edifying. Sometimes people were flogged from one end of town to the other, tied to a cart, with onlookers counting the lashes to make sure the right amount was given.

There was a 'ducking stool' set up in 1653, which had to be repaired in 1718. The ducking stool was for ducking people into the water. In the trial of Florence Newton, she was threatened with 'the water punishment'.

There were other public punishments. Stocks were used – obviously well used – as four pairs were mended in 1673. There was a pillory cage in 1618, meaning a frame with holes for the head and hands, that was locked around an individual, and a new pair of 'finger stocks' ordered in 1684. The stocks were likely to be located in a public area like the square, near the cross. There were other punishments. Soldiers might be billeted in a house to bring pressure on the house owners to conform and there were lesser punishments such as fines, branding, removing the right to vote, the right to trade and other rights.

Richard Gough was elected as mayor in 1614 but refused to take the office. He was fined for this. He took up office a few years later. A number of people were summoned to court for a variety of offences, giving a picture of life, values, customs of the time:

James Sheares, an innkeeper was selling tobacco for a penny a pipeful and he did plead guilty.

Ellen Magner and John Chambers were both charged with keeping misrule in their respective taverns.

John O'Leighy was summoned for throwing the contents of a chamber pot into the street.

Several innkeepers were charged with selling inaccurate measures. Buying quantities of wine but not being prepared to sell any of it was another offence.

John Shanahan paid more than the agreed market price for a pig.

Daniel Comyn bought two shiploads of timber and wood and sold them without permission.

Edmund O'Brien's wife and Margaret Orniell (O'Neill) were both charged with being scolds.

Elizabeth Silvester was charged with being a scold, a thief and an incontinent woman.

The widow Cooney was charged for having a bastard.

John Wilson, the bailiff, had failed to keep the quays clear of dung and had not repaired the battlement of the quay wall.

David FitzWilliam had failed to keep the Water Gate area clean.

The widow Sheffield had blocked the gutter under Tynte's Castle and the consequent pool of water made it difficult for people to pass.

THE ALMS HOUSES

Richard Boyle paid for six alms houses to be built in Youghal to house poor veteran soldiers and left money for the soldiers by way of pension. The houses vary slightly in one respect – the four on the main street have a different roof to the two on the side street, which retain the original style. The doorways seem very small by today's standards – but don't assume people were smaller. Boyle *wanted* people to bow their head going in and out of doors. There is a little ramp up into each house. He *wanted* them to know they were poor and should be humble.

To be fair to Boyle he also paid for a free school and schoolteacher for the town, although sometimes a few years might elapse before a teacher was replaced. Boyle also built fifteen castles (not forgetting the three tombs for himself and a few for his friends), established ironworks, employed 4,000 workers, built up the new town of Bandon, developed Clonakiltyand rebuilt the cathedral of Lismore.

THE RED HOUSE

The Red House is one of the architectural delights of the town, lovingly restored by its owners and today representing one of the very few remaining examples of this style by the Dutch architect Leuventhen. The impressive town house with its wonderful façade, was built around 1705, during the reign of Queen Anne as a home for the Uniacke family.

It has some features that are particular to this style. There are no window sills and pelmets were made of pewter. The bell pulls, the wall panelling, the fireplaces, everything is as it was originally. It looks as if it is a four-storey house, but there are also three mezzanine floors in between, making a total of seven floors and a large, very private garden area to the rear. It was originally built with two wings – one on either side. Today one of the wings is the Old Imperial Hotel.

No self-respecting mansion would be complete without its very own ghost and the elderly lady ghost whose presence is felt in the Red House is a welcome figure who leaves people with a sense of wellbeing and peace. She also tidies up clothing. It has been suggested that she was a nun in her earlier human manifestation, as originally there was a convent next door.

After the Uniacke family the house changed hands a few times. It was a police barracks for a while. It became the home of the parish priest in the early twentieth century. It perhaps reflects the growing prosperity of the Irish people after the Great Famine that the parish priest could live in such a fine house. Some of the back garden was sectioned off and three houses were built on it for the Catholic clergy.

Claud and Patricia Cockburn were frequent visitors. Her book – *Figure of Eight* and his book *View from the West* describe their life in Youghal. Patricia grew up in Myrtle Grove and was herself an author and artist. Claud Cockburn, incidentally, wrote a fine little booklet –*Tourist Trail, a Sign-Posted Walking Tour of Youghal, Co. Cork*, which is hard to find today but is a lovely little book worth reading.

THE TOWN HALL

The Town Hall of Youghal is also known as the Mall Arts Centre. It was originally called the New Rooms. It was built in the late eighteenth century and has seen much of the history of Youghal unfolding. There was a reading room, a ballroom, a coffee house, a meeting place for the Protestant Association, an assembly room, a billiards room and a backgammon room. Famous people like Daniel O'Connell and Charles Stuart Parnell addressed the people from here. In modern times the main room has been used as a theatre. It was commandeered by the army in times of high tension in the early twentieth century.

A beautiful conservatory at the rear offers magnificent views over the harbour, the sailing boats, the occasional visits from wandering dolphins – and is a great place to shelter if it rains.

The Town Hall was also used in the making of the film *Moby Dick*, as it became the costume room for the cast and the production centre for the crew. Over the years it provided the backdrop to the social highlights of peoples' lives – for theatrical events, balls, dances, concerts, weddings and especially public meetings and, more recently, weddings. The beautiful, sprung, ballroom floor is still in use today and a variety of activities take place in this lovely building.

TYNTE'S CASTLE

This was originally built by the Walsh family and later became the property of Sir Robert Tynte. It is one of a number of Tower Houses that at one stage could be found in the town. Tynte married Elizabeth Boyle who had already been married twice. Her first husband was Edmund Spenser, the famous English poet who wrote some of his poetry in Youghal while visiting his friend Raleigh. Tynte and his wife are buried together in the little ruined church of Kilcredan.

The castle itself has played a role of the life of Youghal, especially in the turbulent years of the Wars of the Two Kings (James and William) which effectively ended at the Battle of the Boyne. In the years 1689–90 the Corporation of Youghal was replaced with people more sympathetic to the Catholic cause. The new council elected one

of the Ronaynes as mayor. There was widespread anger among the Catholic population, especially those who had lost possessions after the Cromwellian Settlement. The restoration of the monarchy, they felt, was their chance to have revenge and recover their losses.

Many old Cromwellian soldiers were locked in the castle and angry mobs outside threatened to burn them alive. The mayor, Nicholas Ronayne, managed to calm the situation and save the lives of the prisoners, who were held in the castle for over a year.

After the defeat of the Jacobite army at the Boyne and the Treaty of Limerick was signed, a Protestant Corporation quickly took control of the town. To signify gratitude to the Ronaynes, it was ordered that whenever a Ronayne died the bells of the town would toll. That practice continued until the twentieth century.

ST MARY'S COLLEGIATE CHURCH

This is probably the single oldest church in Ireland to be in constant use over the centuries. It is an architectural gem. The original roof is still there and dates to around the year 1200. In those days the Normans would erect some pillars, build a boat-like structure, turn the boat upside down and – suddenly– there was a church. Like many Christian churches it faces East-West and is cruciform in shape. Several side chapels were added over the years. For a small town like Youghal it made a huge statement of intention when it was built in the late twelfth and early thirteenth century. It was then and remains now a very large church.

There are many features of the church which are fascinating, like the medieval acoustic vases, the tomb of Sir Richard Boyle, the ancient mason stone marks, the curious grave of Elizabeth Scrope, the unbroken list of clergy from 1220 to the present day, the amazing story of Princess Penelope Carolina de Borbone, the tragic First World War crosses, the brilliant heraldic symbols, the medieval heating system and lots more.

There are several chapters in the story of this venerable old church. The State now owns the building, maintains it and ensures it is preserved for posterity, while the local Church of Ireland community continue to use the church for services.

MYRTLE GROVE

There has been some doubt in the recent past about whether or not Walter Raleigh ever actually lived in Myrtle Grove. The confusion is reasonable as the building is referred to as 'The College' and so is the building second next door to it, with St Mary's Collegiate church between the two. One was possibly the residence of the warden of the college, while the second was probably the college itself. The name 'Myrtle Grove' was not used until the nineteenth century.

We know Richard Boyle lived in the building called 'The College', not the building called 'Myrtle Grove'. The question remains – where did Walter Raleigh live? Clearly most of the occupants of Myrtle Grove believed it was the house of Raleigh. David Kelly suggests actual proof is weak but does not suggest a better alternative.

Boyle bought it from Raleigh and then leased it to Sir Lawrence Parsons. The following year, Parsons was appointed Recorder of Youghal. A few years later, the Parsons family departed to live in Birr Castle, but have retained links with Youghal ever since.

In 1670 the house was sold to John Atkins who left it to his grandson, John Hayman. In 1814 it was sold to John Wakefield Pim and then in 1870 to Sir John Pope Hennessy, whose family sold it Sir Henry Blake in 1893 when he retired. His daughter Olive married Major Arbuthnot, his aide de camp.

Sir John Pope Hennessy paints a vivid picture:

… I am resting for a few weeks in 'Sir Walter's study' – in the same room where he looked at the charts of Verazzano before his voyage, and where he first smoked tobacco on his return. The room is much the same as it might have been in those times. The original painting of the first governor of Virginia is there, and a contemporary engraving of Elizabeth, Queen of Virginia. The long table at which he wrote, the oak chest in which he kept papers, the little Italian cabinet, the dark wainscoting with fine carvings rising up from each side of the hearthstone to the ceiling, some with Raleigh's seal, the original warrant, under the autograph and signet of Queen Elizabeth granting a pension to the Countess Elinor of Desmond, and the two bookcases of vellum bound and oak bound books of the fifteenth and sixteenth centuries – for there is nothing in the room (except the writer of these lines) that was not born when Raleigh lived here …

It seems like a fitting room in which Raleigh might entertain illustrious guests like Edmund Spenser who composed part of his poem *The Faerie Queen* in Youghal, or Thomas Harriott, William Shakespeare and Christopher Marlowe.

Sir Henry Blake, as Governor of Hong Kong, accepted a gift of the Golden Gates to Kam Tin which the British Army had captured. Blake installed them in his garden at Myrtle Grove. However, when peace was declared between China and Britain, the Chinese sent a delegation to Youghal to ask Blake's widow for the gates. She agreed on condition that a replica set be made. This was agreed and she returned the gates to the Chinese.

Olive Arbuthnot died in 1953 and is buried with her husband in front of St Mary's collegiate church. Her daughter married Jack Bernard Arbuthnot, a major in the Scots Guard. By a curious coincidence Major Arbuthnot was involved in the Tower of London in 1916 when Roger Casement was a prisoner there awaiting trial for treason. Arbuthnot was a skilful portrait artist and did a number of sketches of Casement in the Tower. Exactly what his role was in the Tower is not known – Casement's family contacted Downing Street to find out where he was being confined and suddenly an army officer contacted them, told them where he was and that he would personally bring them in. That officer was Major Arbuthnot.

Casement at that point had twice attempted suicide and there were two soldiers under orders to supervise him day and night. When Arbuthnot arrived he ordered them to leave and they did. His army records, his involvement with MI5, his activities in the Tower of London are not apparently recorded to any detailed extent or, if they are, are not immediately available for research.

One of the portraits was on the wall in Myrtle Grove but disappeared and was sold at auction. Arbuthnot's son-in-law was the journalist Claud Cockburn who lived in Youghal and mentions the story in his book *I Claud*. His grandson, Patrick Cockburn, also remembers the portrait, and writing in the *Independent* on 1 April 2016, he said:

I had heard about Casement and in a hazy way admired him when I was a child, through a brief but dramatic encounter between my grandfather and Casement when he was a prisoner. He had been arrested on Banna Strand in Kerry after landing from a German submarine three days before the Easter Rising began in Dublin on 24 April. He had been in Germany trying to persuade Irish prisoners to fight against Britain and obtain arms for an insurgency in Ireland.

I knew Casement's name, though not much else, because when I was seven or eight I was shown a drawing of him hanging on the wall in Myrtle Grove, a Tudor house belonging to my uncle Bernard Arbuthnot just inside the medieval town walls of Youghal in County Cork. I was told that the sketch was by my grandfather Jack Arbuthnot, a Major in the Scots Guards who was also an artist and had drawn Casement in his cell in the Tower of London sometime between his arrest and his execution.

THE COLLEGE

In 1464 Thomas Fitzgerald founded Our Lady's College of Youghal, which was something like a seminary today, to prepare young men for the priesthood. In it there would be a warden, eight fellows and eight choristers. As a result of the establishment of a college, St Mary's became a 'collegiate chapel'. As a university it therefore predates Trinity College by some 130 years.

Fitzgerald set money aside to fund this project. Unfortunately, a few years later he was found guilty of supporting the native Irish against the King and was beheaded. During the Desmond Rebellion of 1579–1583 much of Youghal was sacked, including 'The College'. By 1588 The College had been repaired and was then called the 'New College'.

This was the building that Richard Boyle chose as his private residence after he bought the Raleigh estate. He designed beautiful gardens for his house. Sad to say, there was a tragic accident in the garden when one of his children fell into a well and drowned. Boyle moved to Lismore Castle but did return to Youghal, where he died in 1643.

In the eighteenth century the building was replaced by another building. In the nineteenth century it became the home of Leopold Lewis whose property bubble grew and burst.

The finest feature of The College are the magnificent walled gardens, laid out by Boyle and beautifully maintained. It also houses an adoration chapel where prayers are said twenty-four hour a day, 365 days a year.

THE OLD IMPERIAL HOTEL

This is often referred to as the Coach House by locals. It was part of the horsedrawn coach system organised by Charles Bianconi. The entrance to the hotel retains the shape and height of a coach entrance. It has had many names and many owners over the years.

Before the development of a postal service the coaches also brought the mail from town to town. When the roads improved the coach journey to Dublin could be completed in eighteen hours. Eventually the railway system took over the mail delivery function, and that brought with it the demise of the coach service.

The hotel was one of two wings of the Red House before the two were separated.

THE TOWN WALLS

The present town walls form the longest surviving town walls in the country. The walls may look a bit 'thin' but it is to be remembered that they were built before gunpowder and cannons.

In the early *Annals of Youghal* there is a huge concern about the walls. Rebels were constantly attacking the town. There were breaches in the walls and grants were being requested to repair the walls. People were able to slip in and out of town illegally.

At one stage there were thirteen lookout towers in the walls on the land side, while there were two gates into the town from the water side. It was said that the lookouts on the towers would be able to shout to each other and warn them of danger.

ELECTIONS

Public office, especially that of mayor, bailiff or other such dignitary, was carefully recorded. The election of a Member of Parliament was a major event in the life of the town. Up to the mid-1830s the town was considered the property of the Duke of Devonshire, and his nominee for parliament was almost invariably elected. There were eighteen parliamentary boroughs in south Munster, with the Boyle family controlling seven of them. This gave the Boyles huge influence in parliament.

In 1768 an attempt was made by the Corporation in Youghal to change this custom and break the stranglehold of the duke, when Richard Tonson of Dunkettle arrived to support them and 'was ushered into the town by a great number of the independent electors, with colours flying, guns firing, music and other demonstrations of joy, for his timely assistance in support of freedom and independence in the Corporation'.

The attempt failed, probably because a whole raft of new freemen was created which, according to Hayman, swamped the Independents.

By the time of the election in 1833 the political landscape had changed. Catholic emancipation had been granted, and the electoral Reform Act of 1832 changed the system. The Duke of Devonshire no longer owned all of the town. There were now a number of 'Independents' who would reject orders from the duke. John O'Connell, son of Daniel O'Connell, the 'Liberator', was proposed for election in Youghal. There were various legal obstacles, but his wily father had taken care of the property requirements in order to ensure his son was validly proposed.

There was 'dreadful excitement' in the town, so much so that of the 297 registered voters only twenty-seven came out to vote. Twenty-two of them voted for O'Connell. The tiny number of registered votes was surprising, given that the population of the town was almost 10,000 and there were just less than 300 registered voters. The voting was done in public, making it very intimidating either to vote against the landlord's nominee or to vote against an excited 'mob'.

The possibility of a secret ballot did not exist until the Ballot Act of 1872. However, numbered ballot papers made it possible, even with a secret ballot, for those with access to determine who had voted for whom, so that it was not, even after 1872, completely secret.

There was another election in 1835. This time there were 360 registered voters and O'Connell won by seven votes. There was an appeal lodged against the result (described in the *Journals of the House of Commons,* volume 90). It examined the names of all voters and their eligibility to vote. Twenty-eight names were deemed to be ineligible:

Philip Dennehy, James Coppinger, James Sullivan, Michael Leahy, Michael Murphy, Owen Eugene Spelling, James Lynch, Stephen Donovan, Joseph Gibson, William Hayes, Michael Kelleher, Richard Kineary, Henry Thomas, George Baines Heasely, Patrick Cashman, John Murphy, John Power, Edward Croker Giles,

James Kennealy, Thomas Brien, John Clarke, James Campbel, Matthew Blackburn, Jeremiah O'Lomassney, Thomas Murdock Green, Nicholas Purdon Stout, William Flanagan and Henry Elas Roderick.

The list is curious. Some of the names, one might guess, are Irish – Donovan, Lynch, Kelleher but some are definitely more English names. The ineligibility of Nicholas Purdon Stout is intriguing. He was elected chief magistrate in 1838 and mayor in 1840. His family had resided in Youghal since the early 1600s and in 1627 Edward Stoute was Mayor of Youghal.

Having deemed certain names ineligible, the House of Commons did a re-count and O'Connell was declared again to be validly elected. The duke was not pleased.

In 1847 Thomas Anstey became MP for Youghal after another spirited election. A huge public meeting was held on the quay where a platform was erected and several speeches delivered.

A report in the *Cork Examiner* (which included the audience reaction) gave a flavour of the atmosphere:

Now, I will ask every single man amongst you, what the Duke of Devonshire has done to increase the prosperity of Youghal (loud cries of 'nothing').

Yes! Nothing! Our houses are idle, our streets deserted – our stores unoccupied; and look at our lovely harbour, one of the most beautiful in the world, incapable of containing any vessels, the arrival of which would confer an advantage upon our town. (Hear! Hear!)

What benefit is to us that we owe to the fostering care or influence of a nobleman, who taking three of four thousand pounds a year out of his property in this town, never spends a farthing for the advantage of its inhabitants (Hear! Hear!)

His opponent was Mr Charles Ponsonby. People were asked to swear publicly 'I will cheerfully promise and give my vote against the Duke of Devonshire's nominee'.

The Repeal pledge was signed by 112 of the electors. Anstey was not even remotely connected with Youghal, he was introduced simply as an opposition candidate. Mr Curry, agent for the Duke of Devonshire managed the unsuccessful Ponsonby campaign. The duke was even more displeased.

From 1852 until 1868 Isaac Butt was the MP for Youghal. Feelings began to become more and more negative towards the notion of any MP nominated by the Duke of Devonshire. Attitudes in favour of repealing the Act of Union were gaining more and more support. Like Daniel O'Connell before him, and Charles Stuart Parnell after him, Isaac Butt was opposed to the use of violence in pursuit of political aims but still, as a barrister, defended Fenians.

HOW DOES THE DUKE HAVE RIGHTS OVER AN IRISH RIVER?

As can be seen, the increasing number of independent voters in the town led to more and more friction with the Duke of Devonshire. The people of Youghal began to challenge his ancestral rights to the River Blackwater and Youghal Bay. They had failed every time it had come to court.

Way back in 1541 there was a kingly title act brought in to end disputes about land and succession in Ireland. Under Irish law (Brehon Law), there was one system, but under English law there was another. Under English law, for example, the eldest son was next in line. That was no so under Irish law.

In 1541 the vast majority of Irish chiefs accepted the new English law. It is usually called 'Surrender and Regrant'. The Irish chiefs were to surrender and immediately get their land back with an English title. Most thought of it as a simple political strategy, but it proved not to be.

When the Fitzgeralds rebelled they lost their lands, their fishing rights, their title – everything. Walter Raleigh got the land around Youghal, Cappoquin and Lismore, and the rights that went with them, including the fishing rights. When Ireland became a Free State part of the Anglo-Irish Treaty of 1921 stipulated that existing rights (including hunting and fishing) would be respected. This included the rights given to the Fitzgeralds by King Henry VIII, passed on to Raleigh by Queen Elizabeth I. Raleigh sold the town of Youghal to Boyle and all the rights going with it. The Boyle descendants still claim those ancestral rights, dating back to 1541.

CHURCHES

Apart from St Mary's collegiate church, there were two monasteries at opposite ends of the town. The Normans brought with them a number of orders of monks – the Benedictines, the Augustinians, the Dominicans and the Franciscans. Very often they were referred to by the colour of their habits (brown, grey, white and black).

South Abbey was a Franciscan Abbey, perhaps the first one in Ireland, founded in either 1224 or 1231. Little of the original structure remains, but there are pieces of the church in the front gardens of some of the houses around South Abbey.

The North Abbey was a Dominican Abbey, founded in 1268. It was there that the little image of 'our Lady of Graces' was housed. The Benedictines had a priory on the Main Street, where a portion of the gable wall remains. It was probably called St John's priory.

There used to be a convent of St Anne on the Lighthouse Hill. The nuns were in charge of the nearby lighthouse.

After the Reformation, several different Protestant sects were formed. A number of these came to Youghal. Most, if not all, were ex-Cromwellian soldiers.

In Chapel Lane are two churches, including the Wesleyan Methodist Chapel. Both John and Charles Wesley served in Youghal. Their house, on Chapel Lane, is still called Wesley Place. Near their house is the Independent Chapel, built by Protestant Dissenters in 1719.

St Mary's Catholic church on Ashe Street represents the end of the Penal Laws against Catholics. It was built in 1796 and is the first Catholic church to be built in the Cloyne dioceses since the Reformation. Before it was built Mass was said in a variety of places, including the ruined Dominican North Abbey and at a Mass rock on the road called the 'New Line' (which was the scene of dreadful carnage during the Irish War of Independence, see pp.133–5).

St Mary's Catholic Church was initially built with a steeple but this was removed. The grave of Fr Keller, a noted activist in the Land League, is to the front of the church.

The Quaker Meeting House is very close to the Catholic church, as is their main graveyard. The Huguenots did not have a separate church, as they became part of the local Anglican community, which made them even more acceptable.

YOUGHAL PIPE BAND

Youghal Pipe Band is just one of several bands which enriched the town over the years. Christy McCarthy has published a history of the pipe band, but there were so many bands over the years that there is scope for other books to be written.

The band was formed in 1913 in rather unusual circumstances. On one occasion doors to the barracks were 'inadvertently' left open and some instruments disappeared. The following day, Youghal Pipe Band was formed and continues to perform at every major function in the town. The early band members had strong republican affiliations.

A special plaque on the wall in Barry's Lane celebrates the Youghal Pipe Band. Many of the members have served with distinction in the Irish Armed Forces. Marching bands – whether pipe, brass or reed, form an important part of the history of the town.

BOOM AND BURST

As a town, Youghal has enjoyed substantial booms over the centuries and equally devastating economic disasters when the various bubbles burst. During the Napoleonic Wars there was a boom caused by a need to feed the army and navy and a need for timber to build ships. A strong possibility in 1798 of a rebellion in Ireland resulted in regiments of troops from Germany being posted in the town, along with cohorts of the rampaging Wexford militia. There was a strong chance of a French invasion of Ireland, The docks were crowded and the heavily-laden boats departed regularly. There was so much money circulating that the bishop designated Youghal as the main town in the diocese of Cloyne and lived there for a number of years. Then the bubble burst and the bishop quietly departed to the more lucrative town of Cove (later Queenstown and now Cobh).

There was the 'railway' boom and burst story when Youghal was about to become the 'Brighton of Ireland', the River Blackwater would become the Rhine and a whole new era in tourism would develop with Youghal as a major beneficiary. By the 1930s and '40s Youghal was quite poor again. The Quakers had departed from the town but the soup kitchen was reopened and operated by the Red Cross. A 'boot fund' was set up to buy shoes for needy children. Donations of coal were distributed to needy families in quantities of two hundredweight. There was a desperate need for employment.

Paddy Linehan, quoted by Alexander Cockburn, describes the problem faced in Youghal: 'In 1946, I and some other young fellows agreed that we had our freedom all right, but we didn't have freedom from want, from hunger, from unemployment, from malnutrition. There was tremendous emigration.'

Paddy Linehan began to encourage and facilitate economic development in the town by ensuring potential developers were facilitated in every way. The business tycoon, William Dwyer, was looking to expand his Sunbeam Wolsey textile business, and was delighted with his reception in Youghal in 1947 where he promised to build a factory and promote Youghal as a wonderful venue for a holiday. He told the people he would organise a 'Kermesse Week' which would have a golf competition, a bridge competition, raffles and sports. The people were delighted and he took over the 'Strand Palace' ballroom for a full week of free dancing. He also gave twenty-five tons of coal to help needy families.

The 'Kermesse Week' found an Irish name in 1953 and became 'An Tostal'. The local bridge club offered a magnificent trophy for a four-person team, which is still the premier team trophy in the Youghal Bridge Club. A team from Cork won the trophy the first two years. All clubs and societies in Youghal participated in some way initially. The idea was to have a week of festivities in April, thereby extending the tourist season. Gradually the idea declined. Only the bridge club has continued to participate in the Tostal every year since 1953.

Paddy Linehan also met film producer John Huston and convinced him to locate his film, *Moby Dick*, in Youghal. Paddy could offer him the town on a plate, the Town Hall, the streets, the houses – whatever was wanted Huston would get ... and Huston agreed.

William Dwyer set up a company called Seafield Fabrics to make garments of satin and taffeta and lingerie, using a hand-operated loom. The local Technical School offered special training courses in weaving and those who completed the course would be offered employment.

Unfortunately, the first year went badly and share prices slumped. The products were fine, but the county was flooded with cheap imports. By Christmas of 1948 the company closed until such time as the Irish Government could offer protection to the new industry. The government duly obliged and Seafield Fabrics reopened and, with it, Blackwater Cottons.

In 1954 another textile industry opened – Youghal Carpets. The town was soon booming. People had to be bussed into Youghal from nearby towns like Tallow and Dungarvan and a new bridge across the River Blackwater was built. Soon there was employment for over 2,000 people.

William Dwyer lived in the opulent Ashton Court. It was formally the home of Samuel Merrick and later Justin Condon. Merrick had changed the front of a magnificent eighteenth-century house to display the beautiful red brick he was manufacturing, although not all the bricks were actually made in Youghal. Merrick's brick-making business had three big chimneys to fire clay, which created a dense, dull red brick which was well known all over the British Isles. Carts and later lorries carried the finished bricks to the railway station to be transported to Cork and then onwards. Merrick and his brick making business ran into financial difficulty when cheaper imported bricks became widely used. Brick building in Youghal collapsed and Merrick's fine house had a succession of owners until, in 1951, it became the Loreto Secondary School.

For a number of years the town boomed. Seafield Fabrics and Blackwater Cottons employed around 700 people, Youghal Carpets another 350 people and there were ancillary industries like Youghal Sheds and a tanning factory at Green's Quay. Watson's Glass made beautiful stained-glass windows for churches and other buildings. It seemed nothing could go wrong! Three Youghal businessmen even went over to Holland to buy a special river pleasure boat for trips up the Blackwater.

There are a few words that no working person wants to hear – words like 'competitiveness', 'rationalisation', 'redundancy' and very often these words work best together. In the case of Youghal they meant the end of a boom … one by one the textile industries closed as wily business people discovered that many textiles could be made more cheaply in developing countries. In 1993 Youghal

Carpets closed, with the loss of 650 jobs. Before that there had been a number of partial lay offs – with 250 being laid off in 1978.

By 1983 the newspapers were reporting that 2,200 people were unemployed between the two towns of Midleton and Youghal. Similar products could be made cheaper abroad and the government could no longer protect Irish industry from competition. The brick-making business closed down.

In time further industries arrived – including high-tech factories that for a brief spell offered employment such as Artesyn, Kodak, Tytex and others. But they all subsequently left. Paddy Linehan was forever turning sods for new industries, always hoping for the best. In May 2007 Tytex announced it would close, bringing to 2,500 the number of jobs lost in the town in the decade from 1997 to 2007. Boom and burst is the story of Youghal.

4

CURIOUS AND BIZARRE!

GERALD OF WALES (GIRALDIS CAMBRENSIS)

Around the year 1188, Giraldis Cambrensis (or Gerald of Wales if you prefer), visited Ireland and wrote two books about his experiences. He did not do us any favours. Even today the text is so shocking that, in University College Cork, lecturers are usually accompanied by a second lecturer whose function it is to say 'This is not true!' when the comments of Giraldis are being discussed. Sensitive students have been upset in the past at the thought of what he wrote. Essentially he claimed that the Irish were savage, blood-sucking uncivilised barbarians who needed to be conquered. The women were really strange and it was a lawless country.

And, of course, Giraldis's relatives were ready, willing and able to civilise the country and make the inhabitants loyal and decent people. The sons of Gerald (the Fitzgeralds) came in numbers and became as Irish for the Irish themselves, acquiring all the bad habits and none of the good ones, or as it was said, 'becoming too Irish for the Irish themselves'!

There are beautiful drawings to accompany the text, with the originals in colour.

Here are a few of his comments (you can add the 'It is not true!' yourself where appropriate).

- the Irish are a barbarous nation
- some women have beards and hair grows down their back
- the men fight without armour and are very brave

- they don't sow crops
- Some men have intercourse with animals which has led to creatures being born, half man half ox
- some women have intercourse with goats, and lots of children were born with strange defects as a result
- It is an unnatural country where even the cocks crow at different times to the rest of the world
- they neglect their children who, if they survive being abandoned, grow to be very healthy
- they are wonderful musicians
- when choosing a new king they kill a white mare and the new king bathes in the mare's blood and his followers in the flesh,
- many children are not baptised
- they don't have much respect for matrimony and enjoy any woman as they wish
- they are treacherous

In short 'it is indeed a most filthy race, a race sunk in vice, a race more ignorant than all other nations of the first principles of the faith'.

For the next 400 years the text was printed and reprinted and was hugely instrumental in forming the opinion of people about Ireland and the need to conquer and civilise the country.

AN UNUSUAL COURT CASE

Tim O'Neill, addressing the Youghal Celebrates History conference in 2004, related the story of a jealous Youghal merchant, John Don, who, in 1304, believed his wife was cheating on him with a man called Stephen O'Regan. He instructed his servants to follow O'Regan and that if his concerns were valid, they were to ensure that the said O'Regan would never again be physically capable of marital infidelity. His concerns proved to be justified and his servants duly obeyed the instructions they were given.

An outraged Stephen O'Regan, in a somewhat shrill voice, complained that John Don had overreacted and demanded compensation for the undue interference with, and loss of, his personal property, namely his crown jewels. Not to be outdone, Don countersued for the abuse of his personal property, namely his wife, and the consequent loss to him of her affections.

The ruling of the court was that Don had indeed, overreacted and had broken the law in stealing the said O'Regan's personal property, namely, his 'crown jewels'. He was, therefore, entitled to be compensated. O'Regan was awarded £20. However, the learned judge ruled that O'Regan had infringed upon Don's personal property, namely his wife, thereby alienating her affections and therefore Don, also, was entitled to compensation. He was awarded £2, the miserable sum reflecting the belief of the said learned judge that John Don had already got his 'pound of flesh'.

One is reminded of the story of the twelfth-century French monk Abelard who seduced a young girl, Heloise. Her relatives made sure Abelard could never 'do' it again, and in the case of Heloise, she was packed off to a convent. Peter Denman's little poem sums up the ending of the Abelard and Heloise story:

'In time the nun became a proper bitch, and as for Abelard, they raised his snigger to a higher pitch.'

VALUABLE VIRGINS

The Corporation of Youghal was particularly concerned about the behaviour of young men who were engaged in unlawfully interfering with young women. In 1610 they brought in a law to attempt to regulate the situation. Essentially a girl's value was dependent on her family background (which would decide the size of her dowry) and her ability to guarantee the purity of the family name. The only way this could be ensured was if a girl was a virgin on marriage. Unfortunately, some girls were not '*virgo intacta*' because of the activities of the said young men who, the Council believed, should be forced to pay some penalty. The fines would vary but would be cancelled if the young man married the maiden.

This is the transcript from the Council Book of Youghal:

> Whereas divers lewd and incontinent persons, not regarding God or goodness, do through their flatteries and wicked practices labour and endeavour the abuse and overthrow of young and silly virgin maids, to the great grief and discontent of the parents, and to the said young maids' often utter undoing.
>
> It is therefore by the general Assembly provided, that whosoever from henceforth so abuse and deflower any such young maiden virgine,
>
> being a Mayor's daughter shall forfeit the use of the maiden so deflowered, £40
>
> A Bailff's daughter £20
>
> Or any Freeman's daughter £10
>
> And a Groom's daughter £5
>
> Fines to be levied by the Mayor unless the party so offending do marry the said maiden by him so deflowered.

BAD LUCK OR SERIAL KILLER?

St Mary's Collegiate Church has some wonderful tombstones – some are witty, some sad, while invariably all tell a story, like the tombstone of the thrice-wed Susana Russell who died in 1672.

Here lyeth the body of Susana Russell who departed this life the 22nd day of December 1672.

> Interred in Mould here lyeth she
> Who for a time was wife to three
> In constant sorte she lied awhile
> with one whose name was Richard Stile
> When Stile the thread of life had wove
> She wedded was to Stephen Clove
> And with him lied in all content
> Until his glass was also spent
> This virtuous piece, when Clove was dead,
> Did Captain Robert Russell wed
> Where she her virtues did display
> Till death did call, her debt to pay
> Her life on earth with good was blest
> In sweet repose she here doth rest
> Till trump shall sound hence to away
> With Christ to live in blise for aye.

In 1672, Captain Robert Russell inherited the estate of Susana Russell, which included the property of Stephen Clove (her first husband) and the property of Richard Stile (her second husband). The poem refers to the professions of the various husbands – Stile was a tailor and he 'the thread of life had wove' while Clove was a vintner 'until his glass was also spent'.

When she died in 1672, people became very suspicious of Captain Robert Russell. The deaths were a little too convenient – first the two men and lastly the good lady herself and he became quite wealthy.

There was an investigation in 1675 (a few years too late) to examine the inheritances (hers and his) and the convenient deaths. It was impossible to prove anything.

JONATHAN SWIFT

People have often wondered where Jonathan Swift got the grotesque and bizarre idea of writing a story about people selling their young babies as food for educated palates. The answer is, of course, in Youghal! In his *Modest Proposal* Swift offers a simple solution to the problem of the ever-increasing numeric imbalance between Catholics and Protestants. His solution was for wealthy Protestants to eat the Catholic babies.

'Why wait until a child is twelve to sell them as servants to the colonies?', he asks, 'Why not get the Catholics to sell the children at a year old for maybe a fiver a child? With the Catholic propensity for procreation, families could have an annual income and thus solve the problem of poverty, reduce the number of Papists, and solve the nation's woes all in one go. It was, he suggested but a 'modest proposal'. A year-old baby, he argued, made a delicious meal whether roasted, boiled or braised. The leftovers made lovely suppers.

> It is a melancholy object to those who walk through this great town, or travel in the country, when they see the streets, the roads and cabbin doors crowded with beggars of the female sex, followed by three, four or six children, all in rags, and importuning every passenger for alms. These mothers instead of being able to work for their honest livelihood, are forced to employ all their time in strolling to beg sustenance for their helpless infants, who, as they grow up, either turn thieves for want of work or leave their dear native country to fight for the Pretender in Spain, or sell themselves to the Barbadoes.

In University College Cork there are always sympathetic lecturers on hand to reassure sensitive students – 'This is satire, he is joking'. However, there may be more than a grain of truth in the idea. Jonathan Swift went to school in Kilkenny, where he met and befriended William Congreve, whose father was commander of the garrison in Youghal. Congreve senior stayed on after his military career to work for the Duke of Devonshire. Swift became a regular visitor to the Congreves and later bought a house in Youghal.

There are, in fact, two curious entries among the births listed in St Mary's collegiate church – one where the father is named as a 'Jonathan Swift' and the other as 'Dean Swift'.

Captain John Vernon was given a royal commission to enlist children as indentured servants in the colonies. He would offer up to five pounds per child on condition they were 'about twelve years old' but he wasn't too particular and birth certificates were not required. No questions were asked. He sailed from Kinsale to Cork to Youghal and then on to Waterford to fill his quota of children. This amounted to 200 boys and 200 girls.

Families queued up on the quays with their children and assured the captain the child was twelve. Idealistic children were thrilled to be able to help their family by offering to work. The families were thrilled that the child would have a decent job and be fed and have decent clothing. Children were 'signed up' for three to five years as servants in the colonies where the colour of their skin made them more attractive as servants.

They were free after their period of indenture to remain and become wealthy landowners and business people or return home to a life of poverty and misery. Such was the image presented to parents. Few, if any returned. In fact, many died before they served the total amount of their time, living dreadful lives, underfed, overworked and severely beaten for the most minor infringements. They lived in conditions that would have been completely illegal in England.

If Captain Vernon did not fill his quota he was entitled to round up vagrant children and bring them aboard. Sometimes even adults were recruited. Children in Youghal were warned to behave or 'Captain Vernon will take you'. And so, Swift wonders, why wait until they are twelve? Why not sell them at a year? Just a 'Modest Proposal' and the impoverished town he describes could well be Youghal … this being just a modest suggestion.

THE FATA MORGANA IN YOUGHAL

The Handbook for Youghal says there were three instances of a 'fata morgana' in Youghal. This is a sort of superior mirage reflected in the sky. Whether the Youghal version constituted a true 'fata morgana' or not is unclear.

In 1796 a 'fata morgana' was seen in Youghal and ...

> ... this presented the appearance of a hill supporting a walled
> town; on one side of which were houses, and a castle in ruins;
> in the middle were two broken towers, one having a flag flying
> on its battlement; and between them and the castle were more
> houses in ruins. The scene was terminated by a round tower and
> walls. The hill was of a green and brown colour, the buildings
> were purple and brown and the whole had a clear and brilliant
> appearance, like a transparent painting.

What is being described is a very accurate picture of Youghal. The
second time the 'fata morgana' appeared it also projected the image
of the town in the sky. A third fata morgana, which occurred in
1810, depicted an alpine countryside, with hills and snow:

> A third instance of Fata Morgana, which far exceeded the two
> previous exhibitions, was visible at Youghal. About five o' clock
> on a fine morning in June, all the coast on the Waterford side
> of the river was covered with a dense vapour, which presented
> on the right, next the sea, the exact representation of an Alpine
> region. In the background were snow-capped mountains, while
> woods and a cultivated country to the left appeared in front.

THE GHOST OF THE NELLIE FLEMING

The *Nellie Fleming* was the name of a ship that transported goods
between Youghal and other ports, especially Bristol. It was owned
by local coal importer called Martin Fleming. Nellie was the name of
one of his daughters, the other two being called Kathleen and May.

Local historian Mike Hackett gives a detailed account of the
loss of the Nellie Fleming in his book *Lost without Trace*. There
were actually Two *Nellie Flemings* – and both had unhappy ends.
The first ran aground off the coast of Ardmore, where the hulk lies
buried in the sand, occasionally visible after a storm. The second
sank off the Waterford coast with the loss of all aboard.

The *Nellie Fleming* features in a considerable amount of local
legend and folklore about ghosts. She ran aground in Ardmore

Bay in December 1913. Now usually when a ship gets stuck on a sandbank they just wait until the tide rises and the ship floats off. But the *Nellie Fleming* could not float off – there was too much coal on board and the ship was stuck hard. There was some 250 tons of coal altogether.

A local Ardmore man called Martin Fleming offered to buy the ship as salvage. He arranged all sorts of little boats to row out and back, out and back and they got all the coal off the boat and sold it in Ardmore. People came from Youghal and Dungarvan and all neighbouring villages to buy cheap coal from the shipwreck.

Then they took the masts, and the furniture, and the ropes and anything they could take off the boat and then slowly, what was left of the *Nellie Fleming* began to move. It slowly floated off the sandbank and began to drift towards the beach in Ardmore – where she remains under the sand, occasionally visible after a storm.

Martin Fleming bought another boat which he also called the *Nellie Fleming* and it was doing the same job but one night in 1936 just outside Waterford there was a terrible storm and this *Nellie Fleming* sank and all on board were drowned.

In Ardmore Bay there were people out in a small boat and they saw the *Nellie Fleming* coming toward them. The two men in the little rowing boat climbed onto the rocks in Ardmore screaming that the *Nellie Fleming* was coming again into the bay, but when they looked around and the boat had vanished.

They were astonished but they knew it was bad news. One of them got on a horse and rode all the way to Youghal. There were a few people waiting for the *Nellie Fleming*; she was due in about then. When they heard the news, suddenly the whole town 'knew' what had happened and people came out of their houses and knelt down by the quay wall to pray. They did not know then that everyone had died on the ship but they hoped and prayed and prayed. They lit little candles in jam jars and took out Rosary beads and prayed.

Then someone spotted one of the sailors from the *Nellie Fleming* – old Joe Buttimer – everyone knew him – he had a small limp and used to carry a little duffel bag over his shoulder and a rough woollen cap on his head. Everyone knew him but he did not come near the crowd. He went behind the lobster pots and behind the quay over towards Harvey's Dock. His wife ran over, screaming his name, screaming for him to stop but when she got to where he was he had vanished.

They never recovered the bodies from the ship, but sometimes people swear they have seen the crew in the streets of Youghal, with their little duffel bags, heading home. Joe Buttimer in particular can often be seen at night in Youghal wandering the lanes and alleyways on his way home. It helps people who want to see him if they have a good few drinks first.

The Flemings also had another ship – the *Kathleen and May,* which thankfully is still afloat and hopefully will continue to do so for many years to come. Kathleen, Nellie and May were the three daughters of the Flemings. A plaque commemorating the *Nellie Fleming* has been put on a wall near the Town Hall.

SHE'S THE FATHER!

Two young girls presented themselves at the door of a doctor, one of them heavily pregnant. The doctor brought them in and sent for the midwife. He thought they were in their early teens. A few hours later a baby was born. The doctor asked the new mother who the father was and got a most unusual reply: 'She's the father!'

The young mother pointed at the other maid, who blushing furiously, admitted that she was indeed the father. A few questions later the doctor had established that neither girl had any great knowledge of human reproduction. He brought the other girl into a side room where a physical examination proved 'she' was, in fact a fully functioning male.

The doctor sent for the boy's mother who explained that when her son was born she feared for his life. She feared he would be forced to join the army, the navy or get involved in illegal activities and in all cases she would lose him. She had the idea of raising him as a girl, and when old enough to get 'her' a job as a maid. She told no one and the child was raised as a girl and believed herself to be a girl. When she was twelve she got a job as a maid in a local big house where she shared a bed with the other maid, the mother of the new born baby. Eventually, in the course of the night, nature took its course and … 'she's the father'.

THE MOST EMBARRASSING MOMENT IN THE TOWN'S HISTORY

There was always a certain rivalry between the sailing community of Youghal and Cork and challenges to meet 'at oar's length' were frequent. This 'friendly tension' led to probably the most embarrassing moment in the history of Youghal in August 1849, when Queen Victoria paid a visit to Cove, now Cobh, on board her royal yacht accompanied by a squadron of her ships.

There was huge excitement. The name of the town was even changed to 'Queenstown' in memory of the royal visit. A committee was set up to oversee the elaborate preparations. Loyal subjects were invited to light bonfires on the hills to welcome the royal visitor. The town council would provide a display of fireworks as never before seen in Ireland.

As always there were a tiny minority of naysayers who described the event as a 'humiliating farce of servility, toad-eating and flunkeyism'.

Instructions were sent out to those interested in taking part in a 'sail past'. Protocol was vital. Yachts were invited to sail in procession past the royal yacht, slowly, majestically, orderly, and then to lower their flag as they passed by, paying homage to her most royal majesty. It would be a solemn occasion. It was especially important to lower the flag as they passed the royal yacht, like taking off the hat in deference to nobility.

In Youghal there was a strong belief that the town should be represented. In fact the town, they believed, had to be represented. A group of intrepid sailors set out to show the world what the town was capable of doing. They would have the world aware of their wonderful seamanship and Youghal would be put on the map. It was an occasion not to be missed!

Unfortunately, things did not go well. They left Youghal on board the *Arab* in good spirits, possibly too many good spirits. The voyage started badly and steadily got worse. They collided with a schooner as they left Youghal. Neither was prepared to give way. There was no great damage done to the *Arab* and they managed to set sail for Cobh after what was seen as a mere hiccup!

As they reached Capel island, a small but clumsy attempt to light a barbecue led to a fire which threatened to engulf the boat. The deck of the *Arab* caught fire but they quenched the flames. It was amazing what pressure full bladders can bring on any fire and, by God!, were their bladders full! They bravely battled on, determined at all costs to see the queen. They would, for Youghal keep the flag flying. Unfortunately these prophetic words would come back to haunt them.

As they reached Cork Harbour there was a problem with a Cork yacht and would also not give way. Certainly it was unthinkable that the Youghal boat would give way to a Cork boat and she sailed on regardless, ploughing into the Cork boat which overturned, dumping two sailors into the water who almost drowned were it not for the valiant efforts of other Cork crews who were highly unhappy with the bull-headed approach of the *Arab*.

The Youghal men were in even better spirits now. That showed those Cork fellows how to sail! Nothing would prevent them from seeing Her Majesty. They then took their rightful place in the procession of yachts, which began to move towards the royal yacht.

A major problem arose when they tried to lower their flag. They fumbled, they stumbled, they were getting closer and closer to the royal yacht but the bloody flag would not go down! And as they sailed past her majesty the flag was still flying. Her majesty peered through her binoculars and was heard to mutter something very like 'the dirty Arab', which was, in no way intended to be racist. She may have been referring to the smoke damage and the sooty appearance of the boat and her crew after the fire. Who knows?

It was a dreadful insult for a yacht to keep her flag flying as she sailed past the queen – why it was almost like that whippersnapper William Penn who refused to take off his hat in the presence of King Charles II and, if her majesty remembered correctly, that man Penn also lived around Youghal. Royalty tends to remember insults like that. Her majesty, apparently, was not amused.

It was sensational news, and Youghal was certainly on the map, but not exactly as the town council might have liked it. As for the sailors, they had a good day and all got home safely.

THE ECSTATICA OF YOUGHAL

Intense religious rivalry broke out in Youghal in the 1840s. The Catholics blamed the Protestants and vice versa. It probably started on this occasion when the good wife of one of the Protestant ministers, Revd Swanzy, decided to help fallen and destitute females by setting up an institution to house females 'whose moral improvement was to be promoted by a perusal of the Scriptures'.

One of the Catholic priests decided that it was totally inappropriate for Catholic girls to be given lessons in scripture by Protestants and that a Catholic version of the same institution was necessary. The well-intentioned Catholic priest, Fr John Foley, decided to establish not one but two institutions in 1839. He negotiated a large mortgage and bought two houses, one for each proposed work of piety. There were several Magdalen institutions being set up all over Ireland. Government funding helped to develop the number and scope of the institutions. The girls did not have to be Magdalens to be admitted. 'Relapsed' or even 'potential' Magdalens or anyone at risk, anyone in need of re-educationor training – all were welcome. The government would pay. No questions asked. In some institutions the girls were given training in laundry work and many were simply called Magdalen Laundries. They continued to operate right up to the late twentieth century. Fr Foley's establishment for young women was to be called simply the 'Magdalene Asylum' (asylum meaning refuge).

In the second house Fr Foley prepared young men for missionary positions abroad. The irony of his efforts was not lost on the local journalists who thought it was hilarious for a priest who was, on the one hand, preparing young men for a missionary position while simultaneously trying to wean women away from the missionary position.

Already Mrs Swanzy had 'enrolled' thirty girls and was busy improving their 'moral situation'. Fr Foley set about finding suitable girls to rehabilitate. The Protestant authorities were unhappy at the idea of a Catholic priest intervening in work already underway. Mrs Swanzy was already doing a fine job. There was friction between the two sides.

One of the girls Fr Foley wished to 'rehabilitate' was a relative of his, Mary Roche. Mary was admitted to the Youghal Magdalen

Asylum. She and two other girls had returned from Cork where they were attempting to earn a living, apparently in the time-honoured profession.

Fr Foley did not have a lot of money and in 1843 the second installment of his mortgage on the asylum was due and he did not have the funds. Possibly Mary knew this. He was, by all accounts a devout well-intentioned man. In 1843, Mary Roche began to display signs of the stigmata of Christ, puncture marks on hands, feet, forehead and side. She lay rigid in bed, completely oblivious to the world. Little drops of blood appeared on her forehead. Her hands and feet were bleeding. Apparently there was also a wound in her side. It was a miracle.

She was soon followed by two other girls. Word began to get out. Visitors wanted to see the miraculous girls. The girls would go rigid, cold, their heads leaning to one side which, Fr Foley explained, was like the dead Christ. He could not explain why one of the 'dead' women needed to be fed bread and milk from time to time, or why they communicated to him in Irish. Corpses don't need food but this girl did. Corpses don't normally communicate in Irish but these girls did.

The news spread. Newspapers began to follow the story. Soon the grounds of the house were full of fervent pilgrims queuing up to see the miracle, which in 1843, was referred to as the 'Ecstatica' as the girls would go into ecstasy, rigid and cold.

Strategically placed collection boxes helped the financial situation for Fr Foley's mortgage. However, this was purely coincidental!

Fr Foley, initially, would not allow non-Catholics to visit the girls as the 'Good Lord', he felt, would not visit the girls in the presence of unbelievers. Members of the temperance movement were very welcome and devout Catholics. More and more people signed the pledge to renounce alcohol. A few 'unbelievers' did manage to slip in as part of a group of visitors. In particular, Revd Aylward slipped in and watched carefully.

His report was published. He was singularly unimpressed. In fact, he thought the cuts looked suspiciously like those of a penknife, and the blood on the forehead appeared to be smeared, with the blood being secreted from the mouth. A girl would fumble by her dress, then speak to the priest in Irish and he would then invite those present to inspect a hand or a foot which would then be found to be bleeding.

Later the rector of St Mary's Collegiate Church, Revd Drew, was allowed to visit. The girls were 'laid out' in separate rooms. Fr Foley would tell the visitors that he had got a sign, in Irish, from one of the girls that her hand was affected and sure enough when the visitors examined the hand it was found to be bleeding. Revd Drew was not impressed.

The local Protestant clergy demanded an immediate independent multi-denominational examination of the case. Fr Foley affirmed it was all true, and his story was supported by another priest. Fr Foley said he even saw the girls levitating.

The Catholic Church authorities conducted their own investigation. They sadly concluded that Fr Foley was being duped by an 'artful sisterhood', and that the girls had, indeed, some method of secreting blood from the mouth to smear the forehead, that the acting was excellent, and the ability to maintain a rigid posture was superb, but that the Catholic Church really did not need 'miracles' to prove its credentials to others.

Fr Scully, on behalf of the bishop, published his conclusion and read it out in the Catholic church in Youghal, which mortified poor Fr Foley. The funding dried up. A heartbroken, and financially distressed Fr Foley went to his grave protesting his earnest belief in the truth of the story. He died, brokenhearted, shortly afterwards. Neither of his establishments survived.

A QUIRKY LITTLE BILL

This lovely little invoice was sent to the Catholic church in Youghal in 1844:

> For repairing Saint Andrew ...... 8 pence
> For repairing St Peter's thumb ...... 4 pence
> For repairing the Virgin Mary and giving her a new child ......
>   3 shillings and 6 pence
> For repairing the Devil, putting a new horn on his head
> and gluing a piece on his tail ...... 1 shilling and six pence

MURDER ON THE TOWN WALLS

There was a strange murder on the walls in 1709, as recorded in the Council Book:

> In this year that unhappy gentleman Mr Spratt was killed when he was thrown off the walls of the town. He acted very wrong in what he did, but was very drunk when he was killed. Several were tried for the murder, first in Cork and later in Dublin.
>
> One said he would have kill'd him, another said he would like to have had, but to the immortal honour of one of them, he said he followed the brother of the deceased for two miles and would have murdered him too, had he been able to overtake him. But he wasn't. Most, if not all, of the disturbances and troubles of this town were owing to that man Spratt. All those tried were acquitted.

Obviously everyone knew who did it and the subtlety of the word 'too' was probably not lost on a very understanding jury! It must have been considered a reasonable end for an unreasonable man.

5

THE GREAT REBELLION (1641–1650)

There are moments in the history of a town that define attitudes for generations, which partially explain attitudes and which, right or wrong, decide the tone of that town. In the case of Youghal the year 1641 was a seminal year. At that time there was a ratio of about three to one of Catholics to Protestants in the town. The two sets would, by the end of the decade, become even more bitterly opposed to each other and the relationship between them would remain very negative, right up to the twentieth century. Up to the 1930s the signs 'No Catholics need apply' were still being hung in shop windows in Youghal.

In 1641 rebellion broke out all over Ireland. It would last until Oliver Cromwell, brutally but efficiently destroyed all opposition. Within Catholic Ireland there is a strong folk memory of the dreadful manner in which Cromwell did this. Within Protestant Ireland, and especially within towns, the memory is quite different.

It was a rebellion by Irish Catholics who wanted to preserve what little they had left and prevent any further inroads into their rights. Initially confined to the north of Ireland, it gradually spread to the whole island. Catholics were hoping to negotiate favours and reversals of land grants. Most Catholics supported King Charles, while many towns, including Youghal, supported parliament. Richard Boyle kept a tight control of Youghal, Lismore, Dungarvan and Bandon by financing his own troops (1,000 men and 60 horse) in these towns.

In 1642 the authorities in Dublin began to gather evidence of widespread massacres by Catholics. There are several claims that the evidence was exaggerated, but what is important is what is believed to be true, and the Protestant community believed there had been widespread massacres. This belief had a profound impact on subsequent actions taken by Protestants against Catholics.

Typically the belief was that there was widespread 'popish cruelty' – including the murder of women and children, burnings of people and property with the express aim of exterminating the Protestant nation.

Richard Boyle in both of his meticulous diaries and in some letters, gives a vivid picture of the scenes he was aware of and the involvement of four of his sons. One of these sons, Kynalmeaky, was killed in the war but before that he displayed, in his father's

eyes, tremendous bravery in the war against popery. In this account Boyle uses a frightening expression when he talks of 'blooding his troops' on a hundred captured rebels, much as a greyhound owner might blood his dog.

> Yesterday they (Rebels) took eight of my English tenants and hanged them up, and bound an English woman's hands behind her, and buried her alive. My second son, Kynalmeaky, commands my new town of Bandon-bridge where he hath found 500 foot and 100 horse but no entertainment or pay. On 18th the enemies approached the Town Walls, whereupon my son with only 60 horse and 200 foot, charged them in the van, they had a bitter fight. Kynalmeaky, with his horse, closely compassed about the hill, charged them in the rear and brake them; there were 104 persons found dead on the ground, whereof five were principal men of note and leaders. There are many of them wounded; he took 14 prisoners, whom he hanged by marshal law at the Town Gate. He brought home one hundred and forty one of the Rebels' arms and two waynes drawn with 8 oxen a piece with their carriage and provisions, which the boy bestowed amongst his soldiers, and never lost a man of his own, only two wounded; and now we have begun to blood ourselves upon them. I hope God will so bless his Majestie's forces here, as when I now write of killing a hundred, I shall shortly certify you of killing thousands, for their unexampled cruelty hath bred such desire of revenge as every man has laid aside all compassion.
>
> Youghal, 25th February, 1641

A number of residents of Youghal gave testimony about their losses during that 1641–2 period. Their testimony (Depositions) are housed in Trinity College, Dublin, and are available on line. Each person stated what he had lost, what kind of debts were owed to him (or her) and the prospect of recovering any of the losses. Along with the Council Book for Youghal and the diaries of Richard Boyle there is a sense of what life was like in the town. The goods that were traded, the debts owed, the debtors, the geographical spread of the trade – all help build a picture of life in the town at that time. Tobacco was very important.

A few of the depositions from Youghal:

Stephen Clove was robbed of goods to the value of £236. This included six hundredweight of tobacco, linen yarn, linen cloth, wool and a pack of feathers. He wasn't too sure of the exact amount of the debts owed to him as most of his papers were in England.

Thomas Clove had four hundredweight of tobacco taken from him and ninety-four barrels of salt. He had a quarter share in a ship's cargo which was lost and he saw no prospect of recovering any of the money owed to him.

Nicholas Stoutt lost over £4,000 from his several farms in Grange, County Waterford. He was owed £2,233 in debts. Many of his farmhouses had been burnt down and demolished. He saw little prospect in recovering any of his losses.

THE SIEGE OF YOUGHAL

The Ferrypoint, that narrow piece of land jutting out into the sea, played a major role in the siege of Youghal during that war. Briefly, those who supported the king were referred to as Confederates. They were commanded by Lord Castlehaven whose forces attacked towns and castles that had declared support for Parliament.

After one brief mutiny in Youghal in 1645, the town declared for Parliament. There was a brief lull in hostilities in 1646, but the following year Youghal was besieged for ten weeks.

Castlehaven's troops mounted earthen works on the Ferrypoint to challenge any ship that might bring supplies to the town and began to pound the town with his large guns. Fitzgerald castles at Inchiquin, Dromana and Templemichael blocked land routes to the town.

Admiral Penn was ordered to break the siege. He had a number of ships at his disposal – among them the *Duncannon*, the *Mayflower* (not the Pilgrim one) and the *Nicholas*. He put the *Duncannon* at the north side of the harbour mouth and the *Nicholas* at the south side and they began to fire on the Confederate troops on the Ferrypoint.

There are a number of accounts of what happened next. Lord Castlehaven says he fired on the *Duncannon*, which exploded and sank with the loss of eighteen lives. Admiral Penn's more colourful account states that a woman secreted herself on board his vessel and found her way to the powder room, the purpose of which she possibly, misunderstood as she lit a candle, thereby causing an explosion, decapitating the unfortunate woman and killing the seventeen men who had followed her to the powder room.

The Confederates now began to fire on the *Nicholas,* which retreated. The Confederates could now have easily taken the town but delayed and delayed and the advantage was lost.

JOHNNY JUMP UP!

The Catholic forces had a brilliant idea for taking the town of Youghal. Richard Boyle's son, Broghill, had left the town to suppress mutinies in other places nearby. Large casks of local cider were delivered to the town. For a town under siege this was a most welcome present.

The cider tended to be kept in old whiskey barrels, which made the drink especially potent. It was called 'Ryley' but is today more commonly called 'Johnny Jump Up', possibly because most people who sample it end up on the floor. Officers of the garrison and troops together enjoyed the unexpected but most welcome gift.

Broghill returned unexpectedly to find two of his Lieutenant-Colonels (Ridgeway and Bannister) so drunk they could not stand. Neither could most of the garrison. He replaced the garrison with more sober troops and the town was saved.

There was a lull in hostilities. Supplies began to reach the town and after a ten-week siege the Confederates gave up.

CROMWELL IN YOUGHAL

There are many local stories of Cromwell in Youghal, who arrived in the town after a devastating campaign in which he captured several towns and many more surrendered to him. He stayed at the old Benedictine Priory near the gunpowder magazine on the main street. He was very visible to the locals. Not too visible though, as he wore a wide-brimmed hat – perhaps to cover all those warts, for which his face was famous. Every morning he would review his troops along the main street.

In December 1649 he attended the funeral service for Colonel Michael Jones in St Mary's collegiate church. The service was at midnight. Cromwell is said to have stood on a cupboard when giving his oration, saying 'I am sure I have lost a noble friend and companion in labour'.

Jones was buried in the Boyle chapel, with full military honours. Some have wondered about the choice of burial place, but it must be remembered that Katherine Boyle married an Arthur Jones – so there probably was some family connection and it is a huge tomb. There is no church record of the burial but the story features in many of the history books.

There is also a suspicion about the death of Colonel Jones and stories say he was poisoned by Cromwell. Other stories question the loyalty of both Broghill and Jones to Parliament. Broghill certainly managed to ingratiate himself back into royal favour in 1660, being an astute politician who managed to stay on the winning side.

One of the actions taken by Cromwell while in Youghal was to order the melting down of church bells – apparently he found it amusing and ordered that, as gunpowder was invented by a priest, it was fitting that the church bells be converted to 'canons'. Samuel Hayman says the order was anticipated by the local people who buried some of the bells before Cromwell arrived. Strange to say, the main doors of the Town Hall in Youghal are protected by two 'canons'.

Cromwell spent the winter of 1649–50 in Youghal and then on 29 May 1650 sailed back to England, leaving from the Watergate, now called Cromwell's Arch.

REGICIDES IN YOUGHAL

There is a curious grave in St Mary's church in Youghal in memory of Elizabeth Scrope. The gravestone conceals an amazing story. The gravestone is currently inside the church but according to the index of graves it was initially outside.

Samuel Hayman in his *Hand-book for Youghal* fills in some of the detail about the location of the grave:

Beneath the east window, on the outside, is the grave of a daughter of Colonel Adrian Scrope, the Regicide. The monument is an upright slab fastened to the wall, having one extremity supported by the ground, and the other shaped into a triangular headpiece. Mrs Blagrave was buried, 4th August, 1738 (Youghal Register). She was but five years old when her father, along with Harrison, Carew, Clement, Jones and Scot, (all having sat in judgment on the late King, and signed his death-warrant) was executed, 17th Oct. 1660.

Hayman's list of regicides is not complete, but the five names he mentions have a direct connection with Youghal, as do a number of others. Daniel Blagrave, the regicide, was probably an uncle of Jonathan Blagrave, the husband of the Elizabeth mentioned on the grave. Scot was married to Grace Mauleverer whose father was another signatory to the Warrant of Execution for King Charles I. The wife of rector Pierce Drew of St Mary's was a direct descendent of Scot.

Living in Kinsalebeg was Sir John Dowdall, whose daughter married Sir Hardress Waller. Waller was another regicide. He was a frequent visitor to Richard Boyle who also stayed in Waller's house in Limerick. The commander of the garrison in Youghal in 1649 was Robert Phaire who was one of the three colonels (the others being Huncks and Hacker) entrusted with the task of carrying out the Warrant of Execution. Phaire had an estate in Rostellan, east Cork. Next to the gravestone of Elisabeth Scrope is the memorial to Captain John Spencer – one of Major Thomas Harrison's officers. Harrison was sent by Parliament to Hurst Castle to arrest the king and was told to bring a strong contingent of soldiers with him.

Harrison was considered the most dangerous of the regicides and the first to be executed. Samuel Pepys recorded in his diary for 13 October 1660:

To my Lord's in the morning, where I met with Captain Cuttance, but my Lord not being up I went to Charing Cross to see Major-General Harrison hanged, drawn and quartered; which was done there, he looking as cheerful as any man could in that condition. He was presently cut down, and his head and heart shown to the people, at which there was great shouts of joy ... this it was my chance to see the King beheaded at White Hall and to see the first blood shed in revenge for the blood of the King at Charing Cross.

Captain John Spencer was killed in the Battle of the Boyne. Charles Spencer, brother of Princess Diana (née Spencer), does not say whether he is related to this Captain John Spencer and there has been some debate about the connection with the poet Edmund Spencer whose widow Elizabeth remained in Youghal after his death.

One of the regicides was John Cooke. He had an estate in Waterford but a Cooke family in Youghal claimed to be related to him and boasted of their connection. When the male line failed, they changed their family name to Cooke-Taylor. Regicides and their families were especially welcome in Youghal, making it a strong puritan town, the kind of town in which witchcraft and evil might be considered to be a very real threat.

6

THE WITCHCRAFT TRIAL

One of the strangest prisoners held in the town prison in Youghal was Florence Newton, an elderly woman accused of witchcraft.

Witchcraft is often fascinating, it is a story played out in many countries – with a remarkably similar series of events. Invariably you hear of people having fits, seeing the flames of hell, getting sick and all because some malevolent woman has 'bewitched' them, has put the 'evil eye' on them. Usually she is an old woman, with a hooked nose, who is believed to be evil and has made a pact with the Devil. Shakespeare's *Macbeth* paints a vivid picture of witches, satanic rituals and unnatural practices.

The Puritans of the seventeenth century seem to have been pre-occupied with witchcraft and the paranormal. One of the abiding legends is that Oliver Cromwell made a pact with the Devil for seven years of victory. He made the pact, it is alleged, on the eve of the Battle of Worcester and, strange to say, died exactly seven years later. There was a preoccupation with heresy – originally directed at dissident Protestant sects like the Quakers in an attempt to purify the Protestant faith and eliminate all traces of Catholicism. Today 'puritanism' is associated with a straight laced, serious religious attitude which rejects such things as bad language, frivolity, lewd behaviour, blasphemy, opportunities to express such behaviour offered by the theatre and Sabbath breaking.

While there were many witchcraft trials during the reign of the Puritans in England, there were very few witchcraft trials in Ireland. St John Seymour in his book *The Puritans in Ireland 1647–1661* says only one formal witchcraft trial took place in Ireland in that period and it took place in Youghal. There was a preoccupation with evil, with the supernatural, with miracles and with a strict enforcing of religious standard beliefs. Any marginalised person, especially a female, was vulnerable to accusations of heresy or witchcraft.

The incident in Youghal brought together two people – Florence Newton and Valentine Greatrakes – in one of the very rare witchcraft trials in all of Irish history. You could mention Alice Kyeteler in fourteenth-century Kilkenny as a possible witch but she never stood trial, although some of her associates did.

There is very little documentation about the trial. It does not feature in the Council Book of Youghal. Like many towns, the Council records for Youghal for the years 1659 to 1666 are missing. We know about the trial because of the records of the judge and a few letters and diaries.

The old Clock Gate (pictured on p. 104) doubled as a prison. From here rebel heads stared from spikes and pirates rotted in chains. This was the public face of justice in the town. Floggings took place on the steps behind it and hangings from platforms outside the windows.

Perhaps the first question you might ask is – who was Florence Newton? Her background is not precisely known. There were Newtons in Youghal for a generation or so around that time. The Index of Deaths for St Mary's lists four Newtons: a 'widow Newton' in 1689, another in 1698, and a Thomas Newton who died from drowning in 1734. A 'Ketteron Newton' died in 1703. There are no Newton births recorded. There are no Newton marriages recorded. Florence Newton was possibly the widow of a soldier or travelling merchant.

Florence Newton went around the town begging. She was a typical marginalised person who seemed to have access to old remedies for ailments, especially female ailments, including monthly problems and unwanted pregnancies. She thrived on her reputation and she seemed to have a mischievous attitude.

She was angry when, one day, a young maid, Mary Longdon, refused to give her a bit of meat from a barrel in which it was being salted. She looked at her strangely, muttering something about the meat. After that, anytime they met the maid would fall into a fit when Florence Newton spoke to her. Fit, convulsions, vomiting – the lot. Strange objects spewed out of her mouth. She said she saw visions of Hell, she felt needles pricking her and objects flew around her room.

Mary Longdon accused Florence Newton of being a witch. Florence's knowledge of secret remedies for various ailments would have been viewed as suspicious and given credence to Mary's claims. Florence also had an ability to 'look' at people and, somehow or other, people felt she had a power over them. This 'look' was called the 'evil eye'. Florence, unfortunately for her, did not deny these claims. She seemed to think it added to her 'credibility'.

Florence was arrested and tortured mercilessly. The authorities had a book to help them identify witches. Stage one involved not allowing her to sleep, walking her endlessly around a room, shouting at her to wake her up. That lasted up to forty-eight hours. Then she was stripped naked and her body shaved all over to search for a secret devil nipple which witches were supposed to have. That nipple would not bleed if a needle was stuck into it. They tried and tried but could not find a spot that did not bleed. At one point they stuck a needle into her thigh but when the jailer pulled at it, it had stuck fast into the chair she was sitting in. She had boiling urine thrown at her, her hands lanced with blades, and, finally, she was threatened with the dreaded water test.

The water test was a horrible torture. The right hand was tied to the left ankle and the left hand to the right ankle. A rope was then passed between the limbs and the 'witch' was thrown into water.

If she was a witch, she floated. If she did not float she was not a witch (but would probably drown). Threatened with the water test, Florence confessed. She confessed to witchcraft, child killing, anything you like! She also named several other people as 'witches'. Normally when that happened the other 'witches' would be arrested and a number of hangings would be undertaken and the witch-finders would move on to another town. They were well paid for locating and identifying witches. Strange to say the number of witches 'found' was directly related to the amount of money available to find them! When the money ran out the witchcraft problem ceased to exist.

THE TRIAL OF FLORENCE NEWTON

This trial has been described in many books. We are very fortunate that the notes taken by the trial judge survive. One of the people involved was Valentine Greatrakes, former Justice of the Peace for Cork under the Cromwellian regime. He had an estate in Affane, upriver from Youghal.

In 1660 he was out of a job when the monarchy was restored and came to see the witchcraft trial for himself. He realised quickly that Florence Newton was using a 'trigger word' to set off the fits. He stopped the trigger word, which upset Florence Newton.

The crunch test for a witch was to ask her to say the Lord's Prayer. One of the jailers, either for fun or otherwise, began to teach 'the witch' how to say the prayer. Everyone knew witches could not say the Lord's Prayer. Florence Newton could not say it. She always missed a phrase or two. This was, of course, conclusive proof she was a witch. She caught him by the hand and thanked him. He suddenly fell down, his left hand and left side went numb and he believed the 'witch' had put a spell on him. He died soon afterwards.

Suddenly a witchcraft trial became a murder trial. And there the trail goes cold. The verdict was not recorded by the judge, so we do not know what happened in the end. We can guess. She was not allowed a defence attorney. There were no defence witnesses. Eminent historian, Samuel Hayman, says she was hanged. Maybe she was but some would doubt this.

Not one of the other women named by Florence Newton was arrested and charged. This would have happened if they believed she was a witch. There was an intriguing death of a 'Widow Newton' in Youghal in 1689, so maybe good sense prevailed.

Valentine Greatrakes underwent a compete transformation. He had what he described as 'a small moment of great illumination' when he realised he could heal people. And he began to heal people, first near Affane, then Lismore, then downriver to Youghal. He was even invited to London to demonstrate his powers to King Charles II who had a particular interest in anyone who could cure scrofula, often called the 'King's Evil', which people believed could be cured by the divine powers of a king.

As for poor old Florence, the legends persist. Forever more she was 'the Witch of Youghal', disappearing into one of the old tunnels beneath Youghal and reappearing outside the walls to pick the ingredients for her magical remedies.

People believed Florence was a witch and were therefore prepared to believe anything about her and perhaps interpret everything that happened as witchcraft. Her ability to 'look' at someone and suggest things to them might today get her a good living as a hypnotist. Being a beggar, a woman, a marginalised person, would help confirm the belief that Florence was not in God's favour. God, in those Puritanical days, favoured good people and punished bad people. A big house, wealth and health were all signs of God's favour.

Florence, herself seemed to thrive on people's fears and was very annoyed when Mary Longdon refused to give her some meat. She had, she claimed, previously helped Mary with her problems. What these problems might have been we can only guess – very likely common monthly female problems, headaches, perhaps even an unwanted pregnancy.

If she was making old remedies it is certain she would have collected rye grass from the riverbanks in order to take the fungus from it. The rye grass fungus, called ergot, was used widely to cure common female ailments. It is still used today in strictly regulated amounts for problems like headaches.

Ergot contains a drug called LSD for short. If the amount of LSD in the ergot increased, the person getting the remedy could experience a bad LSD trip! And the levels of toxicity in the fungus are directly related to the weather. Bad weather increased the levels of toxicity. So you get a bad LSD trip. That would translate into experiences such as needles pricking, flames of hell – and more. If she was using ergot it would also explain why a girl in Youghal would suffer the same symptoms as a girl in France, Germany or America also having a bad 'trip'. It might also explain the geographical spread of witchcraft trials. Rye does not grow everywhere. There is very little rye in the north of Scotland, but a lot in the south. There is a lot of rye grown in Germany. Sometimes entire villages suffered from eating contaminated rye bread.

If she helped a few girls to have a miscarriage she would probably confess to infanticide, as she did, but there is no story of infanticide in the history books. The poor jailer in the story was fearful of his life when dealing with her and when she caught him by the hand he probably had a heart attack or a stroke, but nothing more.

At a time of major social unease about witchcraft, when people were willing to believe almost anything, it is likely Florence Newton was an unfortunate victim of circumstances. The rabid puritanical zeal to eradicate evil and witchcraft probably had a big impact … and, in the days when universities wanted to control all knowledge, being a woman did not help.

7

PIRATES

The word 'pirate' would frighten even the bravest of people and would send shivers down the spine of all who heard it. Around Youghal, as with all seaport towns, pirates were a curse, a regular threat to any person on land or sea. From the earliest times, coastal towns, monasteries and settlements were prone to attack from marauding raiders.

Some pirates had a fleet of several boats and the many inlets and coves around Ireland proved to be a suitable hiding place as they waited for passing ships. Sailors were often captured and forced to join the ranks of the pirates.

Pirates operating from the Scilly Isles were very prevalent and many Youghal merchants reported losses caused by the 'men of war of Scylly' until the English Navy resolved the issue, as the navy does, by burning and destroying the pirate fleet and base. Pirates had strong bases around the Irish coast – one of these being at Dingle in County Kerry. Richard Boyle's son Broghill encouraged Robert Mouton to attack, sack and destroy Dingle.

Des Ekin has a book called *Stolen Village*, which describes a fearful night on 20 June 1631, when a few hundred Barbary pirates raided the little town of Baltimore in West Cork and took every man, woman and child they could lay their hands on and sold them as white slaves in Africa. The pirates were led into Baltimore by a pilot from Youghal.

All along the coast of England and Ireland people were fearful of such raiding pirates who came ashore. Bernie McCarthy covers the same story in a book called *The Pirates of Baltimore*.

The Earl of Cork, Richard Boyle, was attacked by pirates when he was on his way to Bristol. Boyle was a prime target for pirates and the price on his head was supposed to be £4,200. When you

remember that Boyle paid £1,500 for the 40,000 acres Raleigh sold him, that £4,200 would have bought a lot of land at the time. It was a superb ransom if only he could have been captured. His ship managed to escape but the ship behind him, carrying his servants, was not so lucky and was captured.

There were 250 ships ('prizes') captured around the Irish coast between 1642 and 1650, although one Irish source claimed a figure of 1,900 prizes. About one third of ship's captured were English.

Youghal itself was a safe harbour, with plenty of lookouts and armed citizenry ready, willing and able to defend themselves. They were clearly proactive as, in one incident, the people attacked the pirates and captured six of them – Angus and his five accomplices, who were soon hanging in chains from the Clock Gate. Richard Boyle, in a letter to Lord Chichester (dated 11 April 1613) tells the story:

The townsmen of Youghal have lately surprised at the mouth of the harbour one Angas, with five other pirates who were shipped in a new French bottom of 25 tons, in which there were 4 and 5 tuns of Gascoyne wines, whose taking Mr Parsons can at large relate.

Citizens were ordered to be armed and ready at all hours. But the mouth of the harbour was not always safe as Hugh Baker found out when he went to do a bit of mackerel fishing in his small rowing boat. A large pirate ship, captained by the fearsome John Nutt, captured him and took him on board, probably for ransom or possibly as a recruit. They tied his little boat on to the stern of their boat. For the next week Baker saw the life of the pirates up close and personal.

Nutt had a dreadful reputation for ravishing women, for fearlessly attacking ships, followed by plundering and murder. It was said he killed a negro cabinboy whenever he buried treasure to make sure their ghost would haunt the spot. Capel Island out in Youghal Bay was alleged to be one of his favourite spots. He could hide behind the island, bury treasure on the island and could escape easily.

Nutt had three ships at the time of the capture of Hugh Baker. Three hours after Baker was captured by Nutt they captured the ship of Morgan Phillips of Podstowe (Padstow), who at first refused to surrender, but a few cannon balls into his rigging soon convinced him otherwise. They robbed the passengers of their belongings and took the dozen or so women on board, with all available drink, including large casks of brandy, wine and other spirits. Nutt reserved the most beautiful woman for himself, while the crew

shared the others. She was a Mrs Jones from Cork and he kept her in his cabin for his special 'consideration' while the 'upstanding members' of his crew enjoyed the company of the other unfortunate women.

They took another ship three days later, stripping it of provisions, especially beer, wine, tobacco and butter. The following day they took another ship near Lands End. She was bound for Kinsale with fifty passengers. Nutt and his crew robbed the lot and singled out two men, whom they locked in the hold with Hugh Baker. The rest he let free, and he returned to ravishing Mrs Jones while profusely apologising to her that what was happening to her was not *his* fault – it was *the Government's* fault!

He had, he explained apologetically to her, applied for a Letter of Marque, which would allow him to be a sort of 'legal pirate' or 'privateer' as Sir Walter Raleigh was. He was even offering up to £2,000 for a pardon. And the Government was dragging its heels as Governments do. Now, if he had a Letter of Marque all British women would be safe from his attacks, he reasoned. He was willing to obey the law but 'the Government was very slow to respond to my request', he said.

The attitude of the authorities towards pirates was ambivalent. Most of the pirates were former heroes of the British Navy who performed a useful function by attacking foreign ships and those with a Letter of Marque paid 5 per cent tax on their prize money. So a blind eye was turned and, as long as the pirates were not too much of a nuisance, no great effort was made to stop them. Many were granted a 'Letter of Marque'. Occasionally some were less fortunate.

Captain Fleming was hanged from Youghal from the Clock Gate and the body left to rot in chains as a warning to all pirates that they were a nuisance, and earlier poor Angus and his five accomplices also adorned the same place.

Nutt explained to Mrs Jones he would dearly love a pardon or a Letter of Marque and, unfortunately for her, had to continue his piracy until his situation was resolved. He hoped she would understand. He was waiting for a response and perhaps Mrs Jones could help. He asked her to go to see his wife in Apsham, Exeter, to tell her he was fine, working away, now had some money put aside, (there was £500 with the letter) and he urged her to plead more resolutely for his pardon or his Letter of Marque which would allow him to carry on legally with his piracy and he could then go home safely.

The pirates, Nutt included, began to dip into the large casks of wine, brandy and other spirits destined for more refined palates and became gloriously, footlessly, drunk, with some of the women possibly joining them.

Hugh Baker, locked in the hold with the other two men, could hear everything and spotted a chance to escape. When they were all well and truly drunk, they broke out of the hold where they were being kept, clambered down the rope to his rowing boat still attached to the ship and cut themselves adrift. They made their way to Youghal, where Baker gave his account of what had happened (recorded in the Council Book of Youghal, 23 May 1623).

Strange to say Mrs Jones did deliver the letter and the £500 to Mrs Nutt and her three children and assured her he was fine. She encouraged Mrs Nutt to redouble her efforts to get his pardon. Mrs Nutt offered Sir John Elliott the £500 for his pardon and he accepted the 'gift'. The wonderful Mrs Jones then went to London and implored the Government, in the person of Sir George Calvert, to grant him his wish to be a privateer.

Nutt landed on English soil, believing he had been pardoned, but was promptly arrested, tried and sentenced to death. However, Sir George Calvert intervened for Nutt and had him pardoned and gave him his 'Letter of Marque'.

As for the negro cabinboys – we don't know if that story is true or not, or if it happened only once, but the people of Youghal are very wary of going over to Capel Island which is supposed to be haunted and is still considered to be the burial place of the treasure of John Nutt.

Piracy continued in the Youghal area for many years after. In 1762 six ships were taken by a French privateer, while on their way from Bristol to Cork. Some of the passengers were meant to be recruits for the British Army, but the French did not release them and their fate is not known.

8

THE GREAT FAMINE (1845–1852)

The Great Famine is just one of several famines which hit the poor, Catholic population in Ireland. For over 100 years farms had become steadily smaller, with more and more people at risk of starvation. In most of the previous famines, the problem only lasted a few months, but in the Great Famine of 1845–1852 it lasted a few years.

The population of Youghal was about 11,000 before the famine and dropped down to 4,000 a generation later. Basic political philosophy of the time demanded that governments should not interfere with local business. If people were starving, give them work. That way they could buy their own food and local business would thrive.

For those men able to work a number of projects were offered in Youghal. Some of these projects can still be seen. The Court House off Barry's Lane, the Bridewell Prison near the present-day big supermarket, the Slob Bank on the eastern end of town were all Famine Relief Works. Starving and dying men tried to work. If they collapsed there would be other men eager to grab their shovel and get the day's wages instead.

A Quaker women, called Anna Fisher had an idea for helping women. There was a market for lace. She taught some of the local Presentation nuns how to make lace, believing that they would be better able to teach the skill than she was. The nuns carefully studied her work, picked and unpicked the stitches and then offered to teach women how to make lace. This became a lucrative business very quickly as labour was cheap and the demand was great.

YOUGHAL IN THE 1840S

Samuel Lewis, in his *Topographical Dictionary of Ireland*, gives a detailed picture of Youghal in 1839. The population was 11,327. The barracks had accommodation for 180 men and six officers. There were twenty-eight ships registered in the port and trade was good. A mail coach arrived twice a day and there were several stagecoaches to Cork each day. Many of the houses on the main street were in a dilapidated state and the water supply was defective and deficient. The town was beginning to enjoy the arrival of summer holidaymakers.

During the Famine there was a steady increase in 'criminality' as people did everything possible to get food. Youghal was not the worst town affected by the famine if the figures for those arrested for criminal activity is anything to go by, but it is not quite so simple. The prison in Youghal was being built that year and there was no accommodation available in the Clock Gate, which had been the prison.

Daily committals to prison give some idea of the problems faced in towns. The crimes involved were relatively minor – petty theft of food or clothing being a common one.

In 1847 the figures for prison committals from a few towns in the region for the entire year were:

Bandon	3,358
Castletownbere	1,120
Clonakilty	1,564
Cove	1,576
Fermoy	1,828
Skibbereen	2,489
Youghal	286

This gives a daily intake of less than one prisoner for Youghal, although the prison had several cells. A number of auxiliary workhouses were opened in the town and that might have helped to reduce numbers. Prisoners were given work, varying from mild to hard labour. In a year they broke 200 tons of limestone and baked 154,879 loaves of bread, having ground 1,597 sacks of wheat into flour. They made prison clothes and bargain clothing to be sold 'outside'.

The *Cork Examiner* reported a steady increase in evictions all over the county. People fled to the towns, like Youghal, hoping for food, work, shelter, or the workhouse if all else failed.

A couple tried to sell the body of their dead child for medical dissection. A man left his wife, his mother and his four children in a little hut in Ballyvergan Marsh on the outskirts of Youghal as he went looking for food. They were all shivering with the fever. A spark from the fire caught the roof and all six died.

There had been dreadful poverty, leading to illness, starvation and death for many years. A family in Cork Hill were left naked, barely able to crawl on the floor in 1825. The mother had died and the father pawned everything and still they could not manage. Several times a week they did not eat for twenty-four hours. The family was begging for charity. At that time the story featured in the newspapers. Twenty years later things were a lot worse

In one instance a mob of about 5,000 formed. People armed themselves with clubs, shovels, sticks and demanded food for themselves and their families. Shops were boarded up. One source of food, the Quaker Mill, at Kinsalebeg across by the Ferrypoint, owned by the Fisher family, was not attacked. People knew the Quakers were doing all they could with the soup kitchen and other

THE MALL AND MALL-HOUSE, YOUGHAL, A SCENE OF THE LATE FOOD RIOTS.

humanitarian work. The response was strong – the army and the navy were called in. Hundreds of extra troops were drafted in. Navy boats were sent to the river to prevent any crossing by rioters at the Ferrypoint. Mass graves were opened up in anticipation of a pitched battle. The power of the army was sufficient to calm the situation.

During the famine cholera claimed a number of victims and the fever hospitals were filling steadily. The male to female ratio for these hospitals was 100:1.

CRUELTY AND NEGLECT

The workhouse was to take care of totally impoverished people and those incapable of work. They had to be prepared for a diet worse than anything available on the outside. Those who could would be made to work. Families would be strictly divided – men, women, boys and girls were divided into four very separate sections of the grounds, without any contact between them. Discipline was strict and severe for starving people. 'One day on dry rations' was one punishment. Another was to be confined to a darkened cell, eight feet by six. It was called the Black Hole. Punishments varied from a number of hours to days for a variety of offences. There were also two coffins kept in the Black Hole, which added to the sense of claustrophobia.

One man called Patrick Connolly, described in the *Cork Examiner* as 'elderly and skeletal' (he was sixty years old) was brought before the Board of Guardians because he attempted to steal a piece of bread from the dining room. At meal times Connolly was brought passed the dining hall to the church to pray and to reflect on his sin of attempted theft. One day – we are not told how long he was locked in the Black Hole – he fell and hit his head on one of the coffins. When he was found, some time later, he had died. The authorities were charged with murder. The court found them not guilty as they had not 'set out' to kill him, that his falling was accidental and therefore his own fault. They were, however, negligent. His impulse to steal a piece of bread was brought about by his 'ravenous hunger'.

The medical officer from Midleton was sent to Youghal to see for himself. He wrote to the board to say he was coming. Not one member of the board was there to meet him. His report comments unfavourably on the unsatisfactory and negligent manner of the way the Youghal Workhouse was run. His report was 'noted'. Two of the officials in the workhouse were dismissed for cruelty and neglect as a result of the incident, according to the *Cork Examiner* of 18 May 1849. Their dismissal was 'noted'.

There were at the time 1,200 inmates to look after. The main workhouse had a capacity of 800 people but there was such need that auxiliary workhouses were set up to provide an additional 400 places, which was still insufficient. The Quakers set up a hospice on the North Main Street for the dying and continued to serve food from their soup kitchen.

There were complaints of people being refused food unless they attended Protestant religious services. It was not 'board policy' according to the board and therefore, if it happened, it was unauthorised. The complaint was 'noted'. The expression 'he took the soup' became synonymous with changing religion. This does not refer to the Quaker soup kitchen in Youghal.

Another complaint alleged was that people who were tenants had to surrender their homes before being admitted. They knew that, if they did, they would never get them back. The complaint was 'noted'.

Strangely, some did try to abscond, especially younger people. The records of the Youghal Workhouse survive in the Cork County Archives and give a wonderful insight into the life of those inside. The local newspaper, the *Cork Examiner*, covered the story of the famine as did most newspapers of the time. Newspaper accounts were based strongly on political and religious affiliations. One Youghal Protestant group wrote to the *Examiner* (8 December 1843) to complain that Youghal had been a 'flourishing and happy town' when it was under Protestant control but now that 'Popery' was in control the town was seeing the consequences.

One young boy, James O'Brien, caused consternation when he refused to be slapped in class. An angry teacher beat the daylights out of him and then reported him to the board. James O'Brien was brought before the board. Its members were very angry with the boy. James, in their opinion, was wrong and had to be further punished. He had to learn to put out his hand and not cause the teacher to lose his temper. God knows what harm a teacher could inflict on the boy when he was in a temper! James was severely admonished for his action. His name was 'noted'.

ELIGIBLE YOUNG FEMALES WANTED

Girls were needed in Australia and money was available for 'eligible young females'. Bargains were made with sailing ship companies and young girls would be shipped off to Australia as soon as they were, to use a euphemism, 'eligible'. There were major discussions as to what to give these girls when they were leaving. They had to have everything necessary for a long sea voyage. For one group of thirty-five girls they ordered:

> 50 yards of flannel
> 270 yards of grey calico
> 70 yards of towels
> 35 pairs of shoes

Each girl would have a change of clothing and 'whatever was necessary' and, of course, when they left, the girls would be given the customary cup of tea to wish them well.

WORKHOUSE PREGNANCIES

One problem did preoccupy the meetings of the Board of Guardians of Youghal Workhouse, as some of the women managed to become pregnant. These were not the 'girls of the town' who occasionally tried to be admitted, but instead were respectable married women. The board was outraged and puzzled. The building itself was securely managed to prevent any contact between males and females and there were no 'rogue wardens'.

The problem was discussed and all sorts of theories proposed, including 'Divine intervention'. The women were watched closely at night and by day. There was absolutely no way anybody could meet at night. Men were securely locked in one section and women in another. It just was not possible, but it happened, and on more than one occasion.

It took a couple of years to figure it out but it was all eventually discovered and was seen as another Papist plot to subvert the good order of the workhouse. On Sundays all the inmates would be marched off to Mass, in four separate groups – men, women, boys and girls. Wardens would accompany the group to and from the church. There were wardens in front and wardens at the rear of each group. The route was down Cork Hill, over to the church and then back to the workhouse. They were counted on leaving the workhouse, counted at Mass, and counted when they got back to the workhouse.

Onlookers would stand on the footpath to watch the sad procession of miserable human beings shuffling along. Occasionally some person would run through the group from one house on one side of Cork Hill to another house on the other side of the street. Usually a man would run through when the men were passing and a woman would run through when the women were passing. And the same would happen on the way back from Mass. The wardens thought little of it, just some jostling, some high spirits. Always there would be laughter when someone ran across the street from house to house.

And then all hell broke loose when they found out what was really happening. The man or woman running through the group was not the same person who ran out! Workhouse clothing was easily available. A couple might arrange for relatives to take their place in the procession, put on a workhouse uniform and run through the procession, stop quickly and let another person slip out. The 'replacement' would go to Mass and then repeat the process on the way back. True love would find a way. From then on there were strict punishments for inmates not behaving themselves on the way to or from Mass. The Black Hole would quieten them, and put a stop to pregnancies.

9

A GARRISON TOWN

If any gentlemen soldiers or others, have a mind to serve his
  majesty,
and pull down the French king;
if any 'prentices have severe masters,
any children have undutiful parents;
if any servants have too little wages,
or any husband too much wife,
let them repair to the noble Sergeant Kite, at the sign of the
  Raven, in this good town.

These lines from George Farquhar's play, *The Recruiting Officer*,
probably sum up a lot of the worse side of the British Army – where
the malcontents of society, those in trouble with the law, anyone
who just wanted a new life would be facilitated, had to be facilitated
because the war effort demanded enormous numbers of troops,
willing or not. England, technically, did not have conscription,
which meant a lot more undesirables joining the army to get away
from trouble, as opposed to a country where conscription ensured a
greater diversity of entrants.

Before there were organised State armies, most towns created
their own defence forces, as they depended hugely on a strong
military presence to defend them from attack from land and sea.
Initially this was done by voluntary means, as there was no State
army, no barracks and no funding. Everyone took a turn and there
were strict instructions from the Council. In 1619, for example, the
following instruction was issued:

every Housekeeper before Midsummer shall provide sufficient
weapon or munition for the setting forth of man for the strength

of the town, to have a good sword by his side, a colliver or musket upon his shoulder, powder and bullets accordingly: and every man that hath not a piece shall have a good sword by his side, a lance or pike upon his shoulder.

Householders who did not comply were fined forty shillings.

When organised armies began to be used, the towns had to pay for the accommodation and food for the army, along with the horses. The relationship was not always amicable, as the cost of maintaining soldiers, possibly a few hundred horses, and all the human 'baggage' which accompanied an army could be high.

In 1586 the Corporation in Youghal noticed that many people were hiding food in woods and bogs and remote places to avoid supporting the garrison and demanded that every tenant keep, pinned on the back of the door, a written list of food and animals to be available for inspection. In 1598 the Earl of Ormond visited Youghal, found a lot of stores of food, and calmly took the lot for the army. In 1600 Sir George Carew arrived with 900 soldiers and 100 horses and demanded to be housed for three days.

In 1647, for example, the town was ordered to make provision for the stabling and feeding of 300 horses and the accompanying troops for approximately five weeks. This was not easy, as many buildings had suffered during the rebellion, most of the inhabitants had suffered financial losses and the prospect of levying taxes to pay the £50 needed for the troops and the 300 horses was gloomy. Trading was very limited and therefore there were not many ways the necessary funds could be raised. To make matters worse, while the order stated 300 horses, 500 horses arrived. The corporation begged the right to impose taxes on anybody and everybody with any possibility of paying. The inhabitants of the town had their own horses as well, so the streets must have been fairly full of horse droppings.

After the Battle of the Boyne, two regiments of Danish soldiers were sent to Youghal and had to be housed, fed and generally 'looked after'. The Mayor of Youghal pleaded that the town was unable to pay for two regiments, so the Danes made their own arrangements. The troops were told to take what they wanted. And they did, as the Council Book tells us on 31 October 1691: 'Danish soldiers have robbed and violently taken away provisions and goods and with great violence assaulted the people of the town'.

The soldiers knew that they were entitled to demand a daily allowance of 'a gill of Geneva (gin), 24 ounces of bread, two ounces of greens (vegetable), eight ounces of meat, and a pot of beer'.

And they simply took what they were entitled to.

WHITEBOYS

In 1748 the barracks in Youghal accommodated six unmarried officers and seventy-eight unmarried men. Captain Robert Wrey was in command. The major problem they confronted was 'Whiteboys', who assembled at night with white shirts over their clothes.

Some historians suggest that the white colour was a display of support for the deposed Stuart monarchy. In March 1762 the Whiteboys attacked and levelled ditches near Lismore, attacked the town of Cappoquin, and buried some people alive in Affane. They then threatened people in Lismore to make sure they had horses ready for them, which they had. The group of Whiteboys was numbered at about 400. They then went to Tallow, broke open the prison and released the prisoners and finally arrived at the Ferry Point opposite Youghal where: '... they made a large fire, dug a grave, and erected a gallows over it, fired several shots, and at each shot huzzaed'.

Army raids on groups like the Whiteboys resulted in several court cases, executions and other punishments. The army was on high alert for reports of Whiteboy activity and would respond quickly.

ARMY RECRUITS

There was always a need for recruits and few questions were asked before the 'King's Shilling' was offered. In the nineteenth century alone, England was involved in approximately 190 expeditions and wars all over the world. At the start of the century activities included the Napoleonic Wars, followed by the Anglo Russian war of 1807–12, the conquest of Madagascar, the invasion of Java, war with Egypt, Burma, the Kandyan War, the Barbary War, the Crimean

War, the Opium War, rebellion in India, Sudan, Afghanistan, the Boer War and the Boxer rebellion.

There was, of course, trouble in Ireland two, which necessitated an army presence (mainly from the Young Ireland movement, the Fenians and the Land League). Around Youghal there was further tension when Michael O'Brien of Ladysbridge was hanged in Manchester, one of the three Manchester Martyrs. As the nineteenth century progressed elections became moments of high tension, evictions increased steadily and resistance by the people to oppressive legislation strengthened.

There was always a huge need to feed the war machine and Irish troops played a major role in all of the various wars. If there were not enough soldiers, pressgangs 'encouraged people to enlist'.

The recruiting officers would *not* tell soldiers of the dreadful mortality rate, which was up to 67 per cent per annum in the colonies and that garrison duty involved long-term separation from home and the very real possibility of death caused by matters other than actual warfare, including excessive drink, disease, bad food and squalid accommodation.

Posters give some idea of the kind of person they sought to recruit:

> Brisk lads, light and straight and by no means gummy, not under
> 5 feet 5 and a half inches or over 5 feet 9 inches in height. Liberal
> bounty, good uniforms, generous pay! Step lively, lads, and come
> in while there is time!

So men of uniform size and uniform height were what the army looked for. Probably men handy for making uniforms, coffins and rations. A new custom-built barracks for Youghal was undertaken in 1874, although the issue of married quarters for enlisted men does not seem to have been on the plans. The main barracks was built for up to 300 soldiers and four unmarried officers and there was a military hospital. In Youghal there were up to 400 soldiers arriving weekly for their annual musketry training at Claycastle, where they would pitch tents for one or two weeks before moving back to headquarters.

PRESSGANGS

In 1793 the South Cork Militia visited Youghal looking for men – willing or not – to join the navy. They formed a pressgang of some 800 soldiers and snatched every man and boy in the town they could catch and boarded them on the waiting ships. They captured seamen, fishermen, idlers, schoolmasters, joiners, weavers, tailors – literally anyone they could grab and ship off to join the Royal Navy. Presumably every other town in the vicinity of Cove (Cobh) received a similar visit. The war effort had to be fed and no questions were asked.

WHO WAS IN THE ARMY IN YOUGHAL?

The 'army' in Youghal meant a lot of different things to different people. Three distinct categories of men were involved:

– Locally-resident landed gentry, mainly Protestant, for whom the army provided a career for a few years.
– Locally-resident working-class people for whom the army or navy provided one of the few career choices.
– Members of the garrison which was based in Youghal, formed from categories like the two above but coming from another area, consisting of a group of officers and a group of enlisted men.

Attitudes to the army tended to depend on political affiliations – as invariably the army was used to enforce civil order. Soldiers kept order in the streets as carts trundled along carrying people to their execution, the condemned man or woman sitting on a coffin, soon to be used. Occasionally a soldier would allow an onlooker to give a drink to the prisoner to 'help them on their way'. Soldiers also protected the police while they enforced eviction orders. Soldiers were invariably on the government side, against the people.

TRESPASSERS NOT WELCOME!

The following advertisement was placed by Captain Crowe in several newspapers:

Whereas I, Colonel Thomas Crowe, having been duly informed that several atrocious, audacious, night-walking, immature peach-stealing, poaching rascals, all the spawn of thieves and cubs of hell, do frequently, villainously assemble themselves in my boats on the river, therein boating, piping, plunging, fighting, cursing, swearing, Sabbath-breaking, whoremongering and duck-hunting, with many other shameless enormities and illicit acts, that the modesty of my pen cannot express.

This is therefore to give you all notice, reptiles, scoundrels, ragamuffins, poltroons, whoremongers, adulterers, lank-jawed, herring-gutted plebeians, that if you, or any of you, dare set foot on my boats, or any part of my property, I will send myrmidon like tritons, who shall assail you in the deep, and plunge you in the great abyss ...

CLAYCASTLE

Up to 400 soldiers a time would camp at Claycastle for their annual course in musketry, up to the 1960s. Every three weeks a new group of soldiers would arrive – sometimes marching from Dublin for a few days before setting up camp in Youghal. Sometimes they would arrive by train.

Just imagine the effect of this – 400 young soldiers, 94 per cent of them unmarried, arriving in town and marching along with their drummers drumming, pipers piping and colours flying. The local population would stand by the street and applaud the arrival and local shopkeepers would welcome the visitors. Mothers might lock up their daughters and warn their sons to keep away from the recruiting officers who were absolutely brilliant in the way they convinced men (always men in those days) that they could have a wonderful life and get away from the strife or wife, avoid jail if it was hanging over them and become 'real men' with dashing uniforms, guaranteed to win the ladies, and see life all over the world! For those who joined up the goodbyes with their families and loved ones were harrowing, for often they were saying goodbye to someone they would never see again.

'Join up. Be a real man. Impress the ladies. See the world. Take the King's Shilling.' These promise induced thousands to join the army over the years For many the only hope of a job was to join the army or the navy. There was a sense of idealism, a sense of adventure, which encouraged many young Irishmen to join up. Up to half of the troops who fought for the Duke of Wellington were Irish.

In 1947, the *Youghal Tribune* newspaper was begging the government to restore a garrison in the town, while Sinn Féin warned of the moral depravity associated with a military presence and urged the town to reject the army completely, including the regular arrivals of soldiers for rifle practice at Claycastle. The Claycastle firing range had been in use for a few centuries. It consisted of a large mound of earth and in front of it, facing out to sea, there were large targets to aim at. 'Musketry practice' here had been part of many regiments' annual routine. A few weeks in Youghal by the sea was a welcome part of the schedule.

DUELS

Their were many duels – soldier against soldier, soldier against civilian. The film *Barry Lyndon*, partly filmed at Ballynatray, near Youghal, showed excellent examples of these duels and their protocol, and the razzmatazz of the army marches, with Testosterone flying high.

One of these duels in Youghal involved two young officers – Anthony Watters and Hercules Langrishe, who fought over something trivial – the sugar bowl at breakfast or something silly like that. Watters killed his best friend at the duel. Today they are reunited as they are buried side by side in St Mary's collegiate church. Duels, by law, had to take place outside of town – there

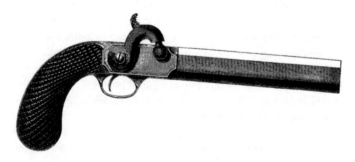

were three main areas Ferrypoint, Rhincrew Abbey and Clifden and as the saying goes: 'Pistols for two, coffee for one'.

Large crowds would go across to the Ferrypoint to watch the duels. Sometimes the crowd might have a few drinks before the duel and on one occasion the ferry overturned due to the rowdy behaviour of the passengers. When the ferry overturned women had a better chance of being rescued – they had hair which a rescuer could pull, while the poor men more often than not did not, or at best did not have enough to pull up!

In reality most duels did not end in death. It was a 'matter of honour', but a man had to 'smell powder'. In fact a man was not a 'real man' until he smelled powder. The guns did not have sights. Deaths did occur but usually honour 'was satisfied' when the two men had discharged their pistols, displaying the utmost courtesy and good manners while trying to kill each other.

In some cases by arrangement, the 'seconds' of those fighting the duel would not put bullets in the guns, and would not tell their two fighters. There is one account of such a duel where one of the duelists knew the pistols were not loaded. The man then pretended to be mortally wounded. His opponent went on the run and a few years later returned to town and was astonished to see the man he had killed walking about.

Duels rarely resulted in a conviction for a surviving participant. Most judges had themselves taken part in a duel. It was a free choice, willingly accepted by both sides. It was part of the process of becoming a 'man'. There were, however, penalties if the duel took place in the town.

SOCIAL LIFE

There was originally no barracks, so soldiers were quartered with the general population. Even when barracks were built, there were no married quarters, so wives and even children shared their accommodation with the unmarried men. Essentially the army did not want married men. Only about 6 per cent of men obtained permission to marry. For the army upper echelons there was a feeling that marriage was incompatible with military efficiency and ought to be discouraged as much as possible. NCOs and soldiers were not to marry without the consent of the commanding officer (a soldier in the Kings Own Regiment was sentenced by court martial to 150 lashes for ignoring this rule in 1828).

> It is the duty of the Commanding Officer to ensure the suitability of the putative wife – that she be clean in her habits, industrious, frugal and not a nuisance.
>
> Any soldier's wife found drunk or disorderly or spreading malicious rumours or bringing liquor into the Barracks will be turned out of the Barracks forthwith.
>
> Duties of wives to include foraging, cooking, laundry, needlework and nursing.
>
> The wives and children will attend medical inspection once a week or oftener if required.
>
> The women and children will attend regularly their respective places of worship. An Absence Report will be sent in every Monday morning by the Quartermaster.
>
> Any soldier's wife who disturbs the Barracks or who is dirty in her habits or who does not behave respectably will be turned out of the Barracks.
>
> A Punishment Book for Barrack Women is to be used to document offences and punishments. Punishments for wives could include branding and flogging.

For wives who had to share the same accommodation as the men, a section could be curtained off. A typical barrack room had fifty beds. If a soldier received permission to marry, one soldier would leave his bed and the bed would be given to the new wife. In 1857 only twenty out of 251 military stations had separate married quarters. There were no married quarters in Youghal initially. When married quarters were provided for, there were regular inspections for the soldiers and their families and punishments were handed out if everything was not in order.

The problem with wives was that there was not enough work for several women – and the army did not want idle women around. Idle women meant 'trouble'. While 94 per cent of men remained single, they were not necessarily celibate. Soldiers were taught the distinction between the various categories of women, and there were really only three: wives, whores and prostitutes.

Whores enjoyed the company of men, may have dispensed favours and may have developed relationships with the men but – significantly – *not for money.* Prostitutes offered a professional service, no strings attached, to the soldiers. Soldiers needed to distinguish between these categories so as not to cause trouble or offence later.

It was not as simple as that, as often soldiers developed romantic links with a woman and then found they were moving to a new barracks, or moving overseas. Sometimes a young girl would get pregnant and follow her soldier in the hope of marrying. The accounts of what happened to soldiers who married without permission are pretty brutal. When soldiers were transferred, there was no provision for bringing a wife, no accommodation for her and no place for her on board ship.

So social life involved mainly single men heading into town with three things on their mind – not necessarily in any particular order – drink, gambling and women. There were many instances of women coming into the barracks to meet men and officers tended to turn a blind eye on this – as long as they did not marry or were too obvious about what they were doing.

And in town there were all sorts of places to facilitate the unmarried, enlisted men who would want some 'female company' and a drink or three. Between ships arriving in port and soldiers arriving in town for recreation Youghal was a busy town at night.

In 1880, 38 per cent of all soldiers admitted to the Curragh Military Hospital were suffering from a sexually transmitted disease. This was often seen as being the fault of the women, of course. The Government introduced legislation to prevent the spread of 'contagious diseases' and set up hospitals where women could be confined if found to be 'unclean'.

YOUGHAL IN 1882

In 1882 the regiment in Youghal was the King's Liverpool Regiment which had a young, underage boy among the ranks. The boy, who was actually Scottish, enlisted under an assumed name. At the end of his tour of duty he went home and did not return when the call went out. He never got the call, as the name he gave was false. His real name? James Connolly, one of the 1916 Easter

Rising leaders.

The army presence meant an enormous amount to the economy and to the social life of the town. In 1881 there had been many incidents:

Four murders
Ten assaults on police
Thirty fires
Two homes burnt, four more attacked
Six houses commandeered
Seven robberies with violence
403 cases of intimidation reported
Thirty-one cases of firing into houses
Three attacks on railway lines
Twelve cases of maiming cattle

There were more and more evictions from the Ponsonby estate near Youghal and the Davis estate outside Killeagh and the army was on full alert all year. The King's Liverpool Regiment was replaced with the King's Shropshire Light Infantry at the end of the year. The population of the town continued to decline from some 11,000 before the Famine to about 4,000 in 1882.

Business was good because of the army presence – there were, on the main street:

Eleven bakers
Six boot and shoe manufacturers
Seven drapers
Twenty-one grocers
Two gunsmiths
Ten vintners
Two pawnbrokers
Nine provisions dealers
Seven general shops
Four victuallers
Two undertakers
Three tobacconists
and W.G.Field, the printing works

It was a busy main street and on the side streets there were shipbuilders, chandlers and rope makers, theatres, two Masonic lodges, schools, several churches and brothels, dressmakers and coal merchants, cabinetmakers and tavern keepers. It was a thriving little town.

The train brought holidaymakers for a day, a week or the entire season. Boats travelled up and down river. In today's terms the presence of the army was probably worth almost €2 million a year to the town. Added to that was the entertainment and sport, the choirs, the regattas, the evening balls, the army parades through town, the army bands marching, the drummers, the army on manoeuvres and the rifle training.

DESERTER! REWARD!

There were always deserters. Some people would 'take the King's shilling' and shortly afterwards desert. Then when the next recruiting officer arrived in town, they would enlist again and again. Descriptions of deserters were very accurate when you consider there were no photographs.

> Notice is hereby given that on the 23rd of February in the year of our Lord 1761 one James Cavanagh from the parish of Pilmore did abscond from the recruiting party at Youghal.
>
> He is by trade a taylor, twenty four years of age, five feet four inches high, dark brown hair, light grey eyes, face lightly marked with foxy coloured beard.
>
> Wears a black wig. He is thin and light but well made. He had on when he went off a grey frock coat, black trimmings, stockings and buckles.
>
> Whosoever apprehends him shall have ONE GUINEA.

The fate of deserters was dependent on the court martial. Thomas McDonagh of the 60th Rifles deserted but was caught. In 1830 he was sentenced to three months imprisonment and to be branded with the letter 'D'. Branding someone on the cheek made it difficult to re-enlist.

However, three militia officers who deserted were treated quite differently, almost humorously as they:

> were sentenced to have their faces blackened all over, and five rations of beef and meal hung about their necks, their coats turned wrong side out, with the label 'desertion' on their backs, and thus to be drummed round the camp three times bare-headed, and then dismissed.

SOCIAL LIFE OF THE OFFICER CLASS

The officers came from the big houses, bought their commissions, and were remembered when they died, because their families could afford it. These officer-class army men tended to be single, spend a few years in the army, perhaps 'sowed the wild oats' and then returned to civilian life to get married and produce the next generation of officers. They were encouraged to wait until they had finished their army service before getting married to a suitable wife. The officer quarters in Youghal was for single men but there was a fine officers' mess, near South Abbey, where officers could meet, eat, drink and socialise. It had a small dance floor and for larger occasions the Town Hall could be used.

For the officers there were regattas, horse races, evening balls, theatrical events, hunting days and all kinds of social occasions to meet desirable young ladies and to display the army costumes which would send these young ladies salivating with desire. They enjoyed a wonderful social life and those officers could drink! At the end of a meal in the officers' mess there were toasts, and each toast involved a drink. In 1824 the following toasts were drunk at one meal:

'To the King!' (drink) (said four times)
'To the Duke of York and the army!' (drink)
'To the Duke of Clarence and the Navy!' (drink)
'To the Duke of Cumberland and the rest of the Royal Family!' (drink)
'To the Duke of Devonshire!' (drink)
'To the Mayor!' (drink)

'To the Glorious, Pious and Immortal Memory of the Great and
  Good King William!' (drink)
'To the Lord Primate of the Church of Ireland!' (drink)
'To the Chancellor, the Bench and the Bar!' (drink)

and there were twenty-five more toasts after that! And twenty-five
drinks!

For the enlisted men, by contrast, they might get a barrel of ale to
share among them, if they were lucky.

LUCY GAULT

William Trevor's beautiful book *The Story of Lucy Gault* captures
vividly the atmosphere of Youghal in the early 1920s. It is a wonderful
evocation of a Youghal long ago – without once mentioning the town!
Trevor called it Enniseala but he is clearly describing Youghal – the
hotel, the lighthouse, the promenade, the firing range. It is all there.
He evokes this wonderful sense of astonishment which permeated
these upper class officers at the thought of being shot at by mere
'plough boys' – officers who had survived the First World War and
now found themselves at home but in a country which had changed
irrevocably since 1916 and which no longer welcomed them. They
became strangers in their own land – like Captain Gault in the story,
wandering aimlessly up the hill towards the lighthouse, down to the
promenade and over to the firing range.

IRISH WAR OF INDEPENDENCE 1921

On 31 May 1921 the 2nd Hampshire Regiment were the garrison in
Youghal and they set off from the barracks to do their usual Lewis
gun practice at the firing range in Claycastle.

The soldiers set out from the barracks led by their military band,
mostly younger men, described in newspaper accounts as 'boys'.
Some accounts describe the subsequent attack as an outrage on
unarmed 'boys' playing music, but eyewitness accounts of the
incident suggest that the band were accompanying troops who were

armed. Flankers in front and to the rear protected the troops but failed to notice an IRA bomb hidden in a pile of stones.

As they marched down what is today called the 'New Line' the bomb exploded, killing seven of the band and injuring twenty-one.

It was a very well prepared ambush with a battery and wiring attached to a bomb that was detonated from some distance away. The bomb killed the bandsmen rather than the soldiers, who were probably the real targets. Remarkable restraint was shown by the British Army after the attack, although immediately following the incident, a local priest was shot while being driven to a sick call by a young man, Patrick Kenure, who failed to stop when ordered to do so. Kenure was also shot dead.

The two bombers were named as two local men, Paddy O'Reilly and Thomas Power, while the bombmaker was Tom Hyde. O'Reilly later fought on the Anti-Treaty side, was arrested and was executed in Waterford in 1923. Tom Hyde fought with the Irish Brigade in the Spanish Civil War (1936–49) and was, apparently, killed by friendly fire. There is no accurate account of the fate of Thomas Power.

It is possible that the attack was part of a reprisal for the destruction of a flying column in Clonmult (in February) that involved the Hampshire Regiment. In the months leading up to this incident there were many others in Youghal. On a number of occasions prisoners who were released by the authorities after spells in jail for republican activities were given a hero's welcome on their return to Youghal. In May 1920 Youghal Bridge was taken over by armed men. On 31 May, a year before the bombing, three Youghal men were released from Wormwood Scrubs Prison and were given a rapturous welcome by the local Sinn Féin and a pipe band, playing rebel music accompanied them to the band headquarters on Cork Hill. The band hall was raided by the military in a search for weapons but nothing was found.

The following night British aeroplanes began to circle the town, searching for illegal activity. There were in the coming months many incidents, some minor, some more serious. There were raids and attempted raids. On 12 July four soldiers pulled down a Sinn Féin flag, apparently without authority. Head Constable Ruddock was shot and wounded in the main street. This was followed by a full military clampdown on all activity, with searches of cars and individuals.

Three young men from Youghal were given two years' hard labour for the attempted kidnapping of two soldiers. There were many searches, most of them fruitless, but a few ammunition dumps were found – one had 950 rounds of .303 bullets according to the *Cork Examiner* of 11 December 1921. One unfortunate shop owner had her name in Irish over the door. This, in the eyes of the authorities, reflected her political affiliations and the shop was searched many times. Known sympathisers were rounded up again and again, sometimes shipped off to Cork but inevitably, returned to a hero's welcome in Youghal. In February 1920 Philip Magnier, Michael Kelleher and Edward Green were all charged with being part of an illegal assembly and sentenced to seven days in jail. William Bland, an ex-soldier, was arrested again and again and each time he returned to Youghal and received an even warmer reception from republican sympathisers.

A statue to Fr O'Neill, celebrating his involvement in the 1798 rebellion, was pulled down one night (17 May 1920).The attack on the statue was very elaborate and was a very well organised affair.

In September and October there was widespread concern and prayer for the Lord Mayor of Cork, Terence Mac Swiney, who, when he was imprisoned in Brixton Prison, went on hunger strike and died there after 74 days in October 1920.

In November an ambush was prepared in Ardmore which led to the immediate death of one soldier and a few weeks later a police constable.

On 11 December Major General Strickland banned all gatherings within two miles of Youghal barracks. Notices were pinned up threatening to shoot 'prominent Sinn Féin members'.

John Cathcart, the managing director of Pasleys Store, was shot dead by the IRA in his own house in March 1921. His death caused widespread outrage. He had recently been widowed and had three young children. A notice was pinned to the body accusing him of giving information to the authorities. A few weeks later a young man, James Quain, who failed to stop when called upon to do so was shot dead.

Eventually there was a peace treaty and the British Army left Youghal. Claud Cockburn says the army could not resist one little dig at the local population when the Treaty was signed ending the war: '... the British military, before they moved out, opened the middle section of the bridge in such a way that when the Irish came to put it back again, the bridge was far from being in a condition as good as new.' This led to the belief that the bridge was unstable and for many years heavy-duty traffic, buses and lorries were not allowed to cross. Lorries were unloaded at one side and all goods transported by hand across the bridge. Passengers left one bus at one side, walked across and got a connecting bus at the other side. However, said Cockburn, this was just a myth and that at night heavy duty lorries did cross. The belief persisted that the bridge could not sustain heavy goods vehicles and eventually a new bridge was built.

10

WHEN HOLLYWOOD CAME TO TOWN

In 1954 a part of the film *Moby Dick* was filmed in Youghal. The film is based on Herman Melville's epic story of Captain Ahab and his, almost psychotic, hunt for a great white whale, called Moby Dick. The story is narrated by Ishmael, a young seaman on board the *Pequod*. Much of the film was made in studio in London, but the most part of the opening sequence was made in Youghal, which for a short few months was made to resemble New Bedford in 1840. The story of how this came about and what actually happened has been told, embellished and retold many times by many people, in particular Michael Hackett.

The almost endless 'credits' (before or after a film) give an insight into the background of a film and give some idea of the work involved in making a film. In the case of the film *Moby Dick* there was a massive amount of preparation for the short few minutes of actual film footage.

Why was it shot in Youghal?

The answer is because writer, journalist and former Youghal resident Claud Cockburn, under the nom de plume Frank Helvick wrote a play called *Beat the Devil* and the film rights were purchased by the Irish-American film director John Huston. The book was made into a film starring many of Huston's actors – Humphrey Bogart, Gina Lollobrigida, Peter Lorre, Robert Morley and directed by Huston himself. Frank Helvick began to write the screenplay but a section of it was completed by Truman Capote, who then got all the credit. During the making of the film Cockburn suggested that Huston make the film *Moby Dick* in Youghal.

Huston came to Youghal, met Paddy Linehan, and agreed with Cockburn that the town could, with a bit of work, resemble New Bedford. It was a gigantic project and the biggest Hollywood budget film to be made in Ireland up to that point. The project involved a huge number of people and in itemising some of them, the scale of the project might become apparent.

PREPARATIONS

Cork Harbour Board met to consider the implications of the film. It would involve dredging the old dock in order to facilitate the 'whaling vessels'. The *Pequod*, for example, was a 350-ton vessel and would require a serious amount of water under her to float. The appropriately-named dredger *Graball* was sent to do this, but was unable to do the job in the small dock area. Eventually the work was done by hand. Teams of men with shovels shifted the tons and tons of sand.

Two Irish Light vessels sailed from Arklow to Youghal to participate in the filming. These were fairly old and not very robust vessels. One was the 75-year-old *Harvest King* and the other was the 73-year-old *James Postletwaite*. The weather was so bad that when they were sailing from Wexford they had to take shelter, but eventually they reached Youghal.

Meanwhile a production crew arrived from England on board the MV *Innisfallen* to oversee the changes to the town. These included an art director, assistant art director, construction director, cameraman, production manager, prop manager and carpenters. There were thirty-six in the initial crew. There was a period of about three months of madness in the preparing of the town for the three of four days of filming. Local builder Michael Murray supervised the set construction from a local point of view.

All kinds of expertise was found, including people like Boonie Flavin, who had sailed deep sea and had great knowledge of rigging and docking. The production crew got bigger and bigger. Money was no object. So much money was spent on the filming that the film did not break even for fifty years.

Local people were interviewed and offered work of all kinds. Every building within sight of the dock had to have a false front to make it look like the wooden houses of New Bedford in 1840. Some houses had a 'widow's walk' installed on the roof, an area where a woman might wait, often in vain, for a family member to return from sea. Hence the name 'widow's walk'. Four of these were required and extra money was offered to the home owners for the inconvenience and the princely sum of £3 extra per house was paid for the 'widow's walk'.

Some of the houses needed a front garden, so sods were taken from fields on the Tallow road to create the illusion.

Youghal Urban District Council leased the Town Hall to the film crew. It became the centre of operations, as well as housing the props and costumes. Costume designers made dozens of costumes for the men, women and children who would be paid substantial money to be 'extras' in the film. Interviews took place to select the extras and hundreds of people applied for the work. There were 100 extras employed. Large hoardings were placed near the Town Hall with lists of those needed the following day. Children were paid ten shillings a day for appearing as extras.

Some fake masts were made. This posed a slight problem because the last masts to be made in Youghal had been for the *Nellie Fleming* back in 1904 when her masts broke during a storm as she travelled from Cardiff to Youghal but on that occasion, she made it safely home. The fake masts were to create the illusion that there were more ships in the harbour than the four that were really there. Newspaper accounts of the size of the masts vary, some said 50 feet, some said 60 feet high but the harbour was to appear to be teeming with ships.

Two copies of most props were made, just in case. Gregory Peck wore an artificial 'peg leg' and two were made. One remained in Youghal in the appropriately named Moby Dick pub. A stagecoach was shipped over from England and two broughams brought down from Bray, County Wicklow There were even two model whales made. These were over 20 metres long, with eighty drums of compressed air and hydraulic mechanisms to move the body parts. Each whale was about 12 tons weight.

The public relations machine began to roll. A special train was arranged to bring journalists from Dublin to Cork and then to Youghal to meet the cast and crew. Journalists from Ireland, England, France and America, along with photographers and others began the journey to Youghal. The American Ambassador, William Taaffe, travelled to wish the project well. Dublin fashion designer Sybil Connolly decided her next collection would have a 'New England' flavour and came to see the film costumes for herself.

An extraordinary exemption from the licensing laws was granted to the entire town so that pubs could be open from 7 a.m. until midnight during the filming. There was intense excitement in the town and autograph hunters were everywhere. Anyone with even a touch of a tan was considered to be part of the film and many bemused visitors found themselves hounded for autographs by hordes of people waving their books.

The most enterprising autograph hunter was local character Rosaleen Cronin, who set about getting the autographs of every major person in the film. The most difficult star to access was Gregory Peck. She first presented herself at the security point to say she had a telegram for Mr Peck. She was not let in. So Rosaleen took a flour bag, cut holes in the bottom for her legs, pulled it up around her neck and suddenly she had a bathing costume. She dived into the water and swam around to the dock area, came ashore and demanded an autograph from a very startled Gregory Peck, who dared not refuse!

There was a special dinner in the Adelphi Hotel, hosted by John Huston. Some of the actors spoke, along with the chairman and vice-chairman of the Urban District Council.   There were lots of speeches. This would be a wonderful moment for Youghal. Employment in the town would be increased, tourism prospects would be improved and in short this would be the 'makings' of Youghal (to sounds of Hear! Hear!).

While this was going on, local auctioneer, Joe Rohan suggested that people might look at the now famous, albeit 75-year-old sailing ship, *Harvest King* which would be available for sale on completion of the film.

THE BIG DAY ARRIVES

By Friday 16 July everything was in place. The big-name actors were ready. The script was ready and the set was ready. Youghal experienced an incredible number of visitors. Over 2,000 cars arrived, extra trains were put on and busloads arrived. An estimated 20,000 visitors arrived to see the production being made. Extra police were on duty to keep the crowds at bay. They could not stop some of the small private planes which flew low over the town to catch a glimpse of the event.

The filming was quite mundane – there was a lot of loading of stores onto the *Pequod* in preparation for her journey. A lot of hens and piglets were needed, and a goat. Captain Holroyd Smith of Ballynatray provided the necessary piglets. Commander Arbuthnot, of Myrtle Grove in Youghal offered the use of his own yacht – the *Three Brothers*, a beautiful two-master which later slipped her moorings in 1962 and foundered on the rocks of the front strand in Youghal.

Most of the Youghal scenes were centred around the *Pequod*. The 'extras' arrived at six in the morning for makeup and costume at the Town Hall. The cast had to be dressed and on set by seven o'clock in the morning and remain there until seven in the evening. During the day a big billboard would indicate who was wanted. Meantime they walked around the town, in costume, proud as peacocks, getting photographs taken and, occasionally, being asked for autographs.

There were 'harrowing scenes' as wives and girlfriends bade farewell again and again to their 'loved ones' heading off to sea, or bustling scenes of goods being loaded on board.

Then the 'extras' or 'artistes' as they were referred to at the time returned to the Town Hall to disrobe and, more importantly, to get paid. Thirty-two shillings and six pence per day, per adult and ten shillings per day per child. It was amazing money at the time and, if the schedule demanded it, overtime was paid was well. Ted Lewis was the financial expert who always had his little box of money ready ... a little over £300 per day being needed. Extras from Cork were brought home in a special bus. Most of these were men, as not enough Youghal men were bearded apparently, causing a slight difficulty as modest Youghal women did not appreciate being embraced by strange bearded men!

By the end of July the filming was over, and the demolition squads arrived to strip the facades of the houses and bring some notion of normality back to the town. The widow's walks were dismantled and the crowd barriers removed. The Town Hall was restored to the council and the special exemption allowed for the filming was stopped, so the pubs returned to normal drinking time.

There was a crew party in the *Showboat* – the local dance hall which was attended by all available members of the cast, including the pet goat which had been staying in the nearby Pacific Hotel.

Regal Cinema,
YOUGHAL.
Phone 63.

We have the honour to present the Republic of Ireland
✳ *Premiere of* ★

'MOBY DICK'
AT A
MIDNIGHT MATINEE,
TUESDAY, 26TH FEB., 1957

Proceeds to be given to The Blind Children of Ireland.

ALL SEATS ARE BOOKABLE AT THE REGAL

Box Office will be Open for Booking on
**Monday, 18th & Tuesday, 19th
February, 1957, from 3 p.m. to
5 p.m. each day.**

"PEQUOD"

Booking by Post will be accepted if the remittance is enclosed.

ADMISSION   -   -   10/-, 7/6, 3/-   (Incl. Tax)

Noel Purcell, one of the Irish stars, sang that night, perhaps the only night in the history of the Showboat that the guest of honour was a goat!

HAVE YOU SEEN A GREAT WHITE WHALE?

Strange to relate, but one of the massive whales constructed for the film broke her tow ropes as it was being towed near Fishguard in Wales, where the filming continued after the Youghal scenes were over. A valiant attempt by one crew member to jump on the whale and secure the ropes failed and the great white whale made a desperate dash for freedom in heavy seas.

The Coastguard and Royal Navy put out an alert asking shipping to be careful, asking various ships if they had seen a great white whale. It was, they warned all shipping, very dangerous. It was some 75 feet long and 12 tons weight but the pressurised air barrels inside the whale could explode. So maybe the whale had a 'boom and bust' moment of its own. In all events the whale was never found.

Youghal returned to normal life and the Town Hall resumed normal service. Paddy Linehan changed the name of his pub to the Moby Dick, where Gregory Peck's famous ivory peg leg is now kept along with lots of photographs and a wall mural painting by Walter Verlin of the town in 1954 when the film was being made.

There is a companion volume to this *Little Book of Youghal* called *Youghal*, part of the *Ireland in Old Photographs* series, also published by The History Press. They go well together. For a greater understanding of life in Youghal over the centuries, read some of the more in-depth books on many of the same topics mentioned in this book.

Also from The History Press

IRELAND IN OLD PHOTOGRAPHS

YOUGHAL

KIERAN GROEGER

www.thehistorypress.ie